EMPOWERED WOMEN'S CIRCLE

For the reluctant woman
who feels called to lead

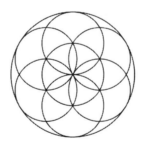

MARIA BROPHY

EMPOWERED WOMEN'S CIRCLE

An easy, step by step format for women's full moon ceremonies with guided meditations and practice exercises to grow love, sisterhood, and wisdom in your community.

Written by MARIA BROPHY

Contributions to this book have been generously gifted with permission by each contributor. Much gratitude for the wisdom shared.

ISBN 978-0-9990115-3-9

First Printing Date: August 1, 2023

Contact the author by mail to: Brophy Art Gallery, P.O. Box 836, San Clemente, CA 92672 USA

Or contact by email by joining Maria Brophy' Inner Circle List here: https://mariabrophy.com/circles

Youtube https://www.youtube.com/@mariabrophy1

Courses www.BrophyArtAcademy.com

This book is dedicated to my beloved soul mate, Drew, who has always supported the sisterhood with love and reverence.

CONTENTS

ACKNOWLEDGMENTS

Much gratitude to all the brave, wild women from times past who risked their reputations, friendships and lives to pass on the secrets of the sisterhood.

I share my most sincere respect and gratitude for the wise elders who came before us, who showed us the way of the sacred circle and how to expand the magic and wisdom of the divine feminine. I honor those who passed down the teachings of the ancients and risked everything to do it.

Thank you to my spiritual mentors, Debi and Alicia, who taught me how to harness my energy healing and gave me confidence to move forward on this spiritual path.

Much love to all my sisters in the San Clemente community and beyond, who consistently show up for healing each month under the full moon. You were there when my Sisters of the Moon Collective companions and I were just getting started with monthly ceremonies in 2021, when we were like newborn does on shaky legs. You gave us encouragement to keep going. You helped us realize that we were making magic, not just for us but for the world.

Words cannot express my heartfelt love and thanks to my friends and family whom I call my prayer warriors and healers, who were there to catch me in 2022 when my husband was dying. You kept my life force intact, and offered me hope. And you gave me the strength needed to help my beloved Drew come back to life, an impossible task that became a miracle.

And finally, I feel so much gratitude for my Sisters of the Moon Collective co-founders, Andréa and Christine. Thank you for stepping out on a limb with me, for encouraging my growth, and for teaching me how to work with a team. You two make my life better. I love that we make magic everywhere we go. I love you girls.

xoxo

INTRODUCTION

My dear lovely sister of the earth,

Women's circles and ceremonies were practiced for thousands of years. And then at one point in history, women were forced to take their ceremonies underground in secret, due to oppression. Today, women's circles are re-emerging across the globe.

A full moon ceremony, a women's circle, or a spiritual circle is a gathering of two or more people who meet to perform rituals that create a strong sisterhood bond and provide healing for all.

My own experience leading women's ceremonies has been profound. I've seen women heal lifelong wounds, break through blocks that kept them stuck, and find empowerment in the sisterhood by giving them courage to take life-changing action.

I wrote this book with the intention of making it possible for you, the reader, to enable my vision of spreading women's ceremonies far and wide to all the little corners of the earth, from the Rocky Mountains to the north shore of the Black Sea, and everywhere in between.

If this book found you, either intentionally as a gift or by accident, it means you are meant to lead the women in your community. Don't let the idea of being a leader scare you. You might be thinking, "What do I know about leading women on a healing journey?" or, "Who am I to do this?" or, "I don't have the right credentials."

Let me stop you right there and remind you why you are on this path. You are a woman desiring to create positive change. You instinctively know that a community is stronger when there is a tribe of women who support each other. You need to be supported yourself. You have a strong longing for something more, something you might not be able to put your finger on that's brewing beneath the surface of your soul.

There, now you have your credentials. This book will show you how to lead the women in your life in a ceremony that will create empowerment, healing, deep connection, and positive change. In the process, you will develop deep lifelong relationships.

I've made it easy for you. All you have to do is follow the instructions and let your heart guide the rest. I'm glad you're here, sister!

CHAPTER 1
BIRTHING THIS BOOK

My name is Maria Brophy, and I am passionate about helping people connect with their inner wisdom and joy.

For over twenty years I've been art agent to my husband Drew. Together we own an art gallery in the small Spanish style beach town of San Clemente, California, just 66 miles south of Los Angeles. Drew and I designed our lives so we could spend a lot of time in nature, backpacking, surfing, and exploring the world.

Before I became art agent to Drew, I worked in the insurance industry for fifteen years. I left that post for the great unknown in the art world. Quitting a stable job was difficult, but the transition upleveled my life from "just okay" to extraordinary.

After I left the corporate job in the early 2000s I was free to expand my growth in public speaking, writing and creativity. It enabled Drew and I to travel the world, sometimes for months at a time. When we were raising children, we took them on those adventures with us.

By 2009 I'd gotten so good at figuring out fun unusual ways to make a living with art that I started coaching artists and sharing my secrets. That led me to author several books on the topic. My best-known book is titled,

Art Money Success, which has helped artists all over the world to grow their art businesses in a non-conventional way.

Although art has been my job for over two decades, I have a great passion for making people's lives happier through coaching and energy healing.

In May 2020, I discovered I could channel wisdom to help others. We were only a few months into the Covid era of lockdowns and isolation, and great fear and depression fell upon many. One day I received a powerful message from spirit to create an online circle of women that would meet weekly to meditate and journal together. I had no idea what I was doing, but I allowed my intuition to guide the way and it helped many women heal, including myself.

I found that spirit was working through me, guiding me on a path that was exciting yet foreign. I wasn't sure how to navigate the flood of intuitive information I was receiving, so I became a student under my first spiritual mentor, Alicia, and began training in Usui Reiki. Though I didn't have an interest in being a Reiki practitioner, I did learn to summon energy healing and I started using it in my coaching sessions with artists and friends.

Energy healing led me organically to facilitating women's full moon gatherings with two of my best girlfriends, Christine and Andréa.

In early 2021, the three of us decided to pool our talents and create a safe space for women to heal and commune once a month. We formed The Sisters of the Moon Collective and started monthly rituals, holding them in my art gallery on the night of the full moon each month.

Andréa provides sound healing with her many magical instruments, and Christine provides Reiki healing during the sound session and leads a journaling exercise coinciding with the energy of the moon. My role is to share inspirational moments and take participants on a guided meditation journey. In later chapters of this book, Andréa and Christine share helpful insights for you on your journey.

Our first few Sisters of the Moon gatherings drew a small number of women, mostly our close friends. Over time, word got out and our numbers grew.

We discovered we were changing lives with this very simple practice. Women tell us how our gatherings provide a safe place where they feel loved and welcomed. Some are healing from divorce, trauma, loss, or illness. Our gatherings give them peace and strength.

One day it hit me that the work we do doesn't just heal our tiny community; it has branched out beyond that. What we have created can easily be duplicated and carried out in other communities by people like you.

The magic in these gatherings is making the world a happier place by empowering women and spreading light and love to everyone who comes. They then take that light and love and spread it in their small pockets of the world, and so on and so on.

At first, I started writing this book to share my channeled guided meditations. But it took on a life of its own. Spirit guided me to transform it into a how-to book to encourage more women to hold women's circles and ceremonies.

My intention is for this book to make it easy for you to step into leadership in your community, one moon at a time. Thank you for spreading the light. I honor you for stepping into a greater version of yourself for the collective. The world needs you!

With great love,

Maria

P.S. Please connect with me in real life. I would love to hear your feedback about how this book helped you create a sisterhood in your community. You can message me on the following platforms:

Join my Inner Circle and get free resources here: https://mariabrophy.com/circles

Instagram @MariaBrophy

YouTube https://www.youtube.com/@mariabrophy1

Courses www.BrophyArtAcademy.com

CHAPTER 2
GREAT MOTHER

*T**his is the Time of the Feminine, our Great Rebirth where women are being asked to steward this next phase of human life where we honor the sacred and protect all of creation.* —**Great Mother**

The following conversation between Great Mother and Daughter is a channelled writing from Shaina Conners, cofounder of Global Sisterhood.

Me: Great Mother?

Great Mother: Hello, my dear daughter.

Me: Why do I feel so unworthy?

Great Mother: Well, I certainly didn't birth you this way. The cause of your unworthiness is a disconnection from me, your mother (Earth) and the great cosmic force within and around you.

Me: So, what happened?

Great Mother: For many thousands of years our Earth has been taken over by parasitic thinking caused by forgetting me and the cosmic unity between all things. This caused many to believe in great scarcity, aloneness, separation, and mistrust. This has gone on for too long and now I am asking my daughters to remember who they are.

Me: Why are you asking your daughters to remember?

Great Mother: This is the time of the feminine, our great rebirth where women are being asked to steward the next phase of human life to honor the sacred and protect all of creation. Through this reflection all beings will be able to walk together in harmony. That's why you need to remember who you are.

Me: How do I begin to feel worthy?

Great Mother: Connect to **who you are** on the inside, in your heart. You won't be able to find yourself in the external world. Learn to believe in yourself and your sisters. Know that you are blessed with unique gifts meant to be used, activated, and cultivated.

Learn to believe in yourself and your sisters.

Gratitude for permission to print this channeled writing from Shaina Conners, cofounder of Global Sisterhood.

Visit @theglobalsisterhood on Instagram or online at www.GlobalSisterhood.org for opportunities to further empower your sisterhood and healing work.

CHAPTER 3
THE RISE OF THE FEMININE

W*e are the wise women returning at this dangerous hour because women worldwide are and always were the guardians of the living earth, as are all the surviving native tribal shamanistic peoples who still commune with the spirits.* —**Monica Sjöö, Great Cosmic Mother**

Long ago in ancient history there was a time when it was a woman's world. Women were revered as healers, wisdom keepers, and the powerful ones. Our intuition is an innate gift, one that communities relied on to keep peace and harmony among the people.

Women were honored for their ability to create life. They were respected for divine intuition that allowed them to tune into nature for answers about healing loved ones. Men viewed their women as goddesses they vowed to protect from physical harm. The relationship between man and woman was equal and symbiotic. There was great peace during this time.

One day darkness entered, and energies changed drastically. Women were stripped of power and punished for accessing intuition. They were burned at the stake for creating healing herbs and concoctions. Religions rose and convinced people that woman's spiritual power was evil. Women were punished for expressing their wisdom, relegated to the "weaker" sex, and dominated by men for centuries to follow. Women collectively learned to hide their intuition and knowledge. They dimmed their lights, hoping to be unnoticed by persecutors. Over time, they forgot how powerful they were, and lost their divine connection to spirit.

This shift opened humanity to male domination, war, and violence, creating a world where more people suffered trauma and abuse. Women and children were no longer protected by their warriors, but instead dominated and preyed upon. The ensuing trauma created a massive need for overall healing of the collective.

The rise of the feminine in the fifties and sixties was the catalyst for a rebirth of women's power. It has taken decades for it to resurface, and now it is here.

The power of the feminine rises strong today. You are a part of this movement. It is your role once again to empower women through sisterhood circles and healing practices. With that healing we create more loving and harmonious communities for all.

This book is a tool you can use to nurture a loving sisterhood circle in your own community.

CHAPTER 4
YOUR ROLE IN HEALING

E*ach one of us has all the wisdom and knowledge we ever need right within us. It is available to us through our intuitive mind, which is our connection with Universal intelligence.* **—Shakti Gawain, Creative Visualization**

My spiritual awakening was first sparked in 1996, when my boyfriend at the time (now my husband) had a book an old girlfriend gave him. He told me the book opened his mind to concepts leading him to create the life he wanted. This caught my attention, because at the time he was living an impossible dream life. Just twenty-five years old, he had an enviable lifestyle traveling the world, surfing big waves, and creating art to support it.

One day he dramatically told me, with hands reaching out for emphasis, "Maria, you can literally create any life you want. It's right here, waiting for you to take it."

At the time, I didn't understand exactly what he meant, but I felt a fire of curiosity and had an inner knowing that he was right. I wanted to learn more. I borrowed the book and read it cover to cover. Many years later I read it to our son as a little boy. To this day, I still have that book on my shelf. I chuckle because the book is inscribed by his ex-girlfriend, "Drew, just a small tool to help you attain all life has to offer. Erin 11-25-1994."

The book is titled, *Creative Visualization* by Shakti Gawain. The book primed me for a massive awakening that came years later in 2006, further opening me to spirit. This happened after a weekend retreat by an organization called The Landmark Forum. It helped me understand why I behave the way I do and how I could transform to who I wanted to be. This retreat ignited a spark that led to massive personal growth and connection to spirit.

What I learned in three days at that retreat was so profound it opened a new world for me. The main lesson from that weekend that made the difference in my life was this:

1. There are things I know that I know (example: I know how make a cake).
2. There are things I know that I don't know (example: I know I don't know how to speak Italian).
3. There are things I don't know that I don't know. This is where the real magic lies in personal growth.

The things we "don't know that we don't know" are the most important answers. To get to those answers, we must be open to new ideas, some of which may sound crazy or impossible.

To be open to new ideas, we must connect to intuition. To do that, we must release some of our set ways of thinking. We must neutralize opinions about what we think we know. We must tell ourselves, "Open your mind to a new way of looking at this."

I invite you right now to open your mind to the possibility of things you don't know that you don't know. With that opening you'll shift to a new world that will inspire you.

There was a time I scoffed at energy healing, the idea that you could generate energy by simply declaring an intention and help heal someone's emotional pain. Then I took training in energy modalities, and witnessed how it helped people.

There was a time I didn't trust my intuition. I thought the "little voice in my head" was just me making things up. Then I learned more and more about accessing intuition and saw how it guided me. I practiced strengthening it, and now I get answers to questions from my intuition that even doctors are unaware of. I've discovered that intuition is always right one hundred percent of the time. Amazing!

There was a time I didn't believe you could communicate with a higher version of yourself, your higher self. Then one day I opened my mind to the possibility. And then I practiced it. Now I rely on my higher self for guidance and assistance with nearly everything important.

Throughout this book I will share things that may help you, also. But first, you need to be open to new ideas. Be open to the possibility that you are fully capable of healing yourself and helping others to heal themselves too.

So, let's talk about healing for a minute. Lately it seems that everyone is talking about healing: energy healing, physical healing, emotional healing, and mental healing. A few years ago, I questioned the idea that everyone needs healing.

"Really?" I would say sarcastically. "Is literally everyone so messed up that they all need healing?"

My logical Taurean mind couldn't agree with this. I knew many people who had great lives, healthy childhoods, and wonderful careers. Surely, they didn't need healing!

Wrong. I came to learn that we all need healing, if not for trauma we've had in our lives, then for what happened to our ancestors, or trauma that happened to the collective.

A collective trauma is one that affects huge groups of people. A collective, harmful lie is one that all humanity suffers from, such as the untruth, "I'm not good enough."

There are multiple collective traumas that everyone is impacted by. For example, indigenous cultures whose entire communities were murdered by invaders. They endured tremendous suffering—rape, murder, decimation of sacred lands. This created a collective trauma passed down through time. Someone with a Native American bloodline may carry trauma from their ancestors without realizing how it affects their life today. This trauma needs to be healed for them to move forward on their spiritual path.

Another example of trauma is one that touches the collective of musicians and artists. For centuries, they've been told there's a specific way to perform, and if they stretch outside that box, they're doing it wrong. There's a voice inside the head of nearly every creative person that says, "You're doing it wrong." The few creatives that break out of the box to follow their intuition and talent make the largest impact on the world. Examples of those you might know of include Picasso, Salvador Dali, Elvis, and The Beatles.

A personal example is the trauma passed down from my great-grandmother, Cecelia Bucek of Slovakia. She was mother to three children in the early 1900s. Her husband left her for another woman, something unheard of at the time. He left the family penniless and humiliated. My grandmother, Caroline Bucek, was one of those three children left behind. She was only fourteen when she was put on a boat to America for a better life. She carried the shame of being scandalized by her father who everyone whispered about. She passed that shame onto her daughter, my mother, Betty Uradnecik. My mother grew up in America with immigrant parents and a very strange last name. She was mercilessly bullied and physically attacked for being a "greenhorn," a derogatory term for Eastern European immigrants at the time.

I was raised by my mother, who had little confidence in herself. She married an extremely abusive man. My father was violent nearly every day. My mother carried guilt for allowing her husband to abuse her five daughters. Shame is a confidence killer. Her shame was passed to me, and I grew up feeling ashamed of who I was. I didn't realize until after my fiftieth birthday that I had carried my mother's shame throughout my life. I also carried her mother's shame, and her mother's mother's shame. And so, on it goes.

Once I realized this, I was able to do healing work that allowed me to release my mother's shame, my grandmother's shame, and my great-grandmother's shame. With that release, I was able to have confidence in doing the things I dreamed of, such as authoring books and giving inspirational speeches to live audiences.

Where do you fit into all this? There's a lot of healing to be done for the collective feminine. You need healing, your mother needs healing, your friends and your community need healing. You can be the catalyst and begin the healing journey for all of them just by holding a women's circle and guiding them in the process I outline for you in this book.

All I ask is that you open your mind to knowing there are things you don't know that you don't know. And in this book, you'll discover a few new things you never heard of. These things will shift you and lift you to your next level of growth. You will be proud to see what you're capable of!

When we heal ourselves, we heal our mothers, our sisters, and our community. With that healing we bring in the light of love and compassion, creating peace and joy for everyone.

CHAPTER 5
ACCESS YOUR INTUITION

I*ntuition is the language of the soul.* **—Candace Thomas, intuitive advisor**

As you step into your role as a leader, your intuition will help you guide more powerful ceremonies by providing ideas and insights.

Every human on the planet was born with a natural superpower called intuition. Some people refer to intuition as messages from spirit, or wisdom from their higher self. There's a lot more to be said about the nuances of intuition versus spirits and guides, but for purposes of this chapter, I'll focus on the basics of intuition.

You've probably heard the famous line in *Star Wars* by Luke. A few times before he ended up in a very dangerous situation, he said, *"I have a bad feeling about this."*

Your intuition is always accurate, one hundred percent of the time. It gives you great insights and wisdom you need in that moment.

Intuition is your natural guidance system telling you which path to take or which to avoid. It's that knowing that makes you think of a friend just seconds before they call you. It's the sick feeling you get in your stomach when you see someone who may be bad for you. It's the great idea that strikes you when you least expect it. It's also that little voice that warns you about impending danger.

Your intuition is an urge, a thought, the sudden strike of an idea that hits you, or a suggestion to do something. Often, we ignore it, usually to regret it later. I'm learning more and more to always pay attention to those urgings.

Just recently I was packing a bag to visit friends for the afternoon. I live in California, where it almost never rains. I suddenly got an "intuitive hit" to grab an umbrella. I laughed because the sun was shining and there wasn't a cloud in the sky. I ignored my urge and left the umbrella behind. An hour later, it started to rain.

Grabbing an umbrella is a small thing. But my intuition has helped me with some very big life issues, like the time in 2016 when I was healing from an autoimmune disease. I had suffered for years as my body functions failed. Doctors didn't have answers, and I felt totally alone.

One morning I woke up and something terrifying had happened to my vision; there was a halo around everything. I could barely see faces and it wasn't safe for me to drive. I was very afraid and prayed for an answer.

One day thereafter I was in my bedroom getting dressed. I was calm and relaxed at that very moment. That's when my intuition spoke. A loud whisper in my ear said just one word, *Ashwagandha.* I looked around and no one was in the room with me. I thought I had imagined it. I had never heard of Ashwagandha; I didn't know what it was.

Then it was whispered in my ear again, two more times, *Ashwagandha, Ashwagandha.* Now I was intrigued. Did I imagine it? I opened my laptop and Googled Ashwagandha and found it's an Ayurvedic herb used to help heal the nervous system. I wasn't convinced it would help, but I was willing to try anything. I went to Amazon and ordered a jar of powdered Ashwagandha. It arrived the next day and I mixed a tablespoon in warm water three times a day. Within a week, my vision cleared. By the time the jar was gone, my vision was fully restored.

Throughout my life before this, I had small experiences of intuition guiding me. But this experience was the most profound, where I actually heard the word in my ear. It gave me confidence that intuition was available to me and I could use it to help when I needed it.

The problem is many of us disconnect from our intuition as children. We are discouraged by well-meaning parents, teachers, and adults to look for answers outside ourselves. In other words, we're taught to look to other people for answers, outside our own inner knowing. Intuition is wisdom that comes from within, and only you really truly know what's best for you.

The great news is that you can train yourself to access your intuition, and as time goes on it will get so powerful and accurate you'll rely on it more than you rely on Google or outside opinions.

Intuition comes through in different ways for different people. You may feel it physically, hear it in your ear, get an inner knowing, a flash of insight, or even "see" things in your mind's eye. You may feel it as an energy shift in your body. Or you may get your message by smelling something.

Some people access their intuition in more than one way. For me, I hear it audibly some of the time, other times I feel it, and sometimes I see the messages in my mind.

You can access your intuition by noticing how you feel when you're around people. For example, a dishonest person may make your stomach hurt or feel bad. This is your inner knowing. Make note how your body reacts to unspoken messages.

When you receive an intuitive "hit" with an idea, warning, or thought, pay attention to it. Give it respect and receive it. The more you notice and receive messages from your intuition, the more it will speak to you.

When you are fully present in your body, intuition comes through easier. When you get quiet, you're more likely to receive your intuition. That's why people come up with the best sparks of insight while in the shower or on a nature walk; there are no distractions, and your mind is clear to receive messages.

Think of intuition as a message being delivered. If you're distracted, scrolling social media, surrounded by noise and other people's energy, the message cannot get through.

How to Access Your Intuition Step by Step

1. Go somewhere quiet where you won't be disturbed.
2. Set aside your phone and all distractions.
3. Take a breath and notice your body. Feel your breath move in and out.
4. Call in your higher self by literally inviting her in and asking her to help you access your intuition. You can say, "*I call in my higher self. Please help me connect to the wisdom of my intuition.*"
5. Ask a question out loud.
6. Listen for the answer. Feel in your body, see in your mind's eye and pay attention. Trust that the answer will come.
7. Notice the very first thing that pops into your mind. Receive the answer when it comes.
8. If the answer does not come within a few minutes, ask out loud for the answer to come to you at the perfect time.
9. Notice when it comes and trust it.

Things That Disconnect Your Intuition

There are things that interfere with your ability to receive intuitive messages. They include:

- Drugs and alcohol
- Toxic people
- Negative news, videos, movies, books
- Scrolling social media, video games or other electronic distractions
- Pharmaceuticals that disconnect you from feeling
- Constant noise, chatter, chaos
- Complaining

Things That Increase Your Connection to Intuition

- Quiet time with your thoughts
- Meditation
- Laughter
- Sunshine and nature
- Exercise
- Psychedelic plant medicine
- Energy healing sessions
- Eating organic fruits and vegetables
- Being around high-vibration people

Practice accessing your intuition daily by getting quiet and asking questions, then listen to receive answers. In the beginning, ask easy yes or no questions such as, "Should I take a jacket?" or, "Should I call that client right now?"

As you get more confidence in your ability to receive answers, you can ask more complicated questions. Once you get stronger at this, answers will come before you finish asking the question. The question should be framed in a way that an answer can be easily given.

Examples of questions you can ask:

"How can I _____?"

"Who should I ask for help with _____?"

"What will it take for me to _____?"

When you receive an answer, you may wonder if it's your imagination or if it's intuition. Below are a few guidelines to help you discern the difference between your own monkey mind and true intuition.

It's **not** intuition if:

- There is fear or judgement in the answer
- It's the second message you received immediately after the first
- The answer keeps you stuck in a belief system
- There was worry, confusion or stress in the answer

It **is** intuition if:

- It was the first answer that popped in
- The answer is calm and peaceful
- It feels safe and trusted
- It is simple wisdom
- It feels right

Sometimes imagination will throw us a message, confusing us between the actual intuitive message and our own monkey mind. One way you know your imagination is at work is when it overrides an intuitive message that goes against your old belief system. This is when you put your lifelong belief system in neutral to receive true wisdom.

For example, I have a strong belief system against taking pharmaceutical products. This is so ingrained in me that when I got an infection after a tooth extraction, I refused my doctor's prescription and took alternative medicines. But the infection didn't go away. I tuned in to my intuition, which told me to take antibiotics. That was something my belief system didn't want to hear, so I fought it. Eventually, I listened to my intuition and for the first time in twenty years I took a round of antibiotics. It successfully healed my infection and prevented me from further health issues.

Intuition is neutral. It does not have a belief system, a political party, or stubborn views. It does not hold grudges. Intuition has the answers to everything, and with great wisdom. To receive it, we have to allow it to flow to us freely, without restriction.

Once you start using your intuition daily, everything will feel easier— your relationships, the decisions you make and the challenges you face. You will never feel alone, since you'll know you have all your answers inside you.

If you're interested in learning more about accessing intuition, there are many books you can read and websites that can help. Look at the reference section of this book for suggestions.

"When you start tapping into your intuition regularly, you will never feel alone. You contain all the answers inside of you."

CHAPTER 6
HOW TO USE THIS BOOK

F ull moons are a potent gateway to enable change in our lives, to let go of unwanted energies and to replace them with something we want.

This book is intended to give you an easily followed format to lead a women's Full Moon Ceremony or Women's Circle. You will find that I use the phrases "women's circle" and "full moon ceremony" and "ceremony" interchangeably in this book.

I've been leading full moon ceremonies since 2021 and for years prior to that, women's circles. The difference between a circle and a ceremony is the format.

In this book I focus on holding your gathering as a full moon ceremony, because that's what I love most and because the full moon is a potent time to gather. However, you may choose to hold your women's circle anytime during the month, and you may change the ceremony to any format that best fits you and your community.

If you're new to leading women's circles, you may want to follow each month's ceremony step by step as laid out for you in this book.

It's best to prepare in advance by reading the moon chapter you plan to follow and then practicing the flow of your ceremony. A little practice and preplanning will make for a smoother event. I encourage you to make changes to the ceremony format by adding your own personality and ideas.

At times when planning for your ceremony, you'll receive inspired ideas from your intuition. These ideas often come as flashes of insight or a strong thought that pops into your head. Notice when this happens and implement the ideas in your ceremony, since they come from a higher source meant to serve your tribe.

In this section I will introduce you to the parts of the ceremony from beginning to end.

Choose Your Date

The full moon has been celebrated for thousands of years in ancient cultures. Full moons are a potent time to create a gateway to enable change in your life, to let go of unwanted energies, and to replace them with something you want. The full moon is believed to be the most powerful time to do spiritual work to release the old and bring in the new.

The energies of the full moon are present the day before the full moon, the day of the full moon, and the day after. That three-day window is the most potent time to do a full moon ceremony.

However, the meditations and exercises given here can be done at any time. If you can't schedule it in the three-day period of the full moon energies, your next best option is during the new moon, or any time that works for you and your tribe.

Research the dates of the full moon and the new moon online and choose a date that works best for you.

I encourage you to schedule an entire year of ceremonies on your calendar. This book gives you twelve months of ceremonies plus bonus meditations and exercises as well.

Gather Your Tribe

A ceremony can be performed with two or more people. Ideally, you'll want to gather a small tribe of women from your community. I find it's best in the beginning to invite your most open-minded friends, those who are searching for something new and not afraid to discover things.

You may want to keep your ceremony small, between four to six friends, and as you get more practice, open it to your community and offer it to more people.

A note about bad energies: some people bring dark clouds into a space. Sometimes these are the people that most need this work! That said, if you have someone who attends your ceremony and brings bad energy by complaining, engaging in negative talk or giving a general bad feeling, you may want to turn them away so they don't spoil it for everyone else. Or you may try to raise their vibration by giving them extra love and an extra smudging! Go with your intuition for the best way to handle people who bring low vibrational energy into the room.

Here I make a note about inviting men into your circle: you may choose to open it to men. However, when men are present it changes the dynamic. Women are less likely to open up, and you will no longer focus on what the divine feminine needs to heal. The ceremony should then cater to the masculine as well as the feminine. This is completely acceptable if you are called to do so. Men also need healing. Go with your heart and what you feel your community needs.

Invite Your Tribe

For your first ceremony, if you choose to keep it small, you may personally invite friends and family who you believe will enjoy it.

You could call, text, or message each person and say, "I'm hosting a women's full moon ceremony on Wednesday from 6:00-7:30 p.m. We will do some healing and I'll guide a meditation. It will be fun! I'd love for you to join me. Can you be there?"

When you're ready to open your ceremony to your community and bring in more people, you can use an online platform such as Facebook, Meetup.com or Eventbrite.com. Set up your event and share links to it by text, posts on your social media, and emails to people you know.

Charge a Fee or Make it Free

You may choose to offer your ceremony for free, or you may want to charge an entry fee or ask for donations. Do what feels best to you.

If you're new to leading, offering a free gathering at first will help you build your confidence level. Sometimes when you bring money into an equation, it makes you more nervous about your performance. I would prefer you make decisions that motivate you to keep taking action and leading these ceremonies. Do what works best for you.

Please know that you can change how you conduct the ceremony from month to month as you gather more experience and confidence.

Collaborating

You may choose to ask one or two friends to help you host the ceremony. If you have a friend who plays musical instruments, you may ask them to perform a song or sound healing. Or, if you have a friend who can lead a gentle yoga session before the meditation it would be a nice addition. Or you can invite an energy healer or Reiki master or any other type of spiritual expert who can bring another feature to your circle.

My ceremonies are hosted by me and two dear friends; we each have our own talents. Christine shares information on the moon cycle each month and guides a journaling exercise. She also gives Reiki energy healing during the sound portion of the ceremony. My musician friend Andréa is a sound healer and energy healer. For each ceremony she brings her crystal bowls and gong, along with other instruments and performs healing music during and after the meditation. My specialty is to share an inspiration and then channel and guide the meditations.

Please know that your ceremony does not need to have a live sound healer, a Reiki master, or anything else. These are added bonuses and may present themselves to you in time. Begin with what you have right now.

Seating, Journaling, and Oracle Cards

Ask your tribe to bring their own yoga mats or cushions to lie on. I have found that meditation is best done lying down for the comfort of everyone. Or you may have chairs for everyone to sit on instead. Older women or those with bad knees or injuries may need a chair rather than a yoga mat. It's important for you to make sure that each person is physically comfortable during the ceremony.

Have small pieces of paper and pens ready to hand out for the journaling exercise.

If you have an oracle card deck, lay it out on a table so everyone can pull a card after the ceremony. Light candles or have LED candles to set a warm mood.

Prepare Your Sacred Space

Before each ceremony, prepare your sacred space. This involves setting up the area for seating, preparing your altar, and cleansing the energy in the space.

First, you'll set up the area where the ceremony will take place. You can do it indoors, in a living room, or any other space where you can comfortably seat the people who plan to attend. You can do it outside, in your yard, in the forest, or on the beach. You can perform your ceremony in a different location every month if you choose. Make sure there is ample room for your tribe to comfortably sit or lie down.

Prepare Your Altar

Next, you'll prepare your altar. This is a small area you will set up at the front of the room or area where you'll be sitting. The altar serves as a focal point and spiritual catalyst for the energy you'll create during ceremony.

Your altar can be small and simple, or it can be ornate. It should include items that represent earth, wind, fire, and water. At a minimum, your altar should have an arrangement of the following items:

- Base for the altar items (this can be a shelf, a small table, a tray, mat, white fabric, or use the floor).
- Items representing fire: white candles, a light, or the word fire written on a piece of paper.

- Items representing earth: crystals, rocks, dirt, plants, fresh flowers or herbs, anything from earth, or the word earth written on a piece of paper.
- Items representing wind: feathers, burning incense, or the word air written on a piece of paper.
- Items representing water: a small bowl or container holding water (extra powerful if the water came from the ocean, a river, lake, or stream), or the word water written on a piece of paper.

Make your altar your own by adding items that mean something personal to you and your tribe.

Here's a list of other items you can add to your altar if you wish: flowers, photo of your favorite spiritual guide, angel or someone who inspires you, abalone shell, small statue representing one of your guides, an inspiring book, handwritten notes with mantras or inspiring words or poetry, a mirror, anything representing abundance such as money or jewelry, anything heart-shaped, oracle card decks, etc.

Take joy in assembling your altar items in a way you find beautiful. Take time to breathe in and out gently, thinking of your intentions for the ceremony as you intentionally and joyfully create your altar.

Set Your Intention

Intention setting is a powerful way to ensure that every single person receives love and healing in a way that makes their lives better.

Your intention can be very specific to the world's current affairs or your community. Or your intention can simply be this: "My intention is to make sure that every single woman who arrives tonight feels great love, acceptance, and joy."

Every monthly ceremony I share in this book also has an intention, and you may use those as well.

Cleanse and Open Your Sacred Space

The last thing you do before your tribe arrives is cleanse your personal energy and the space with smudging. This is a simple clearing of old, stagnant, or negative energy that may be lingering on you and in the space.

This step is incredibly important and cannot be skipped or shortened. Please allow at least ten minutes or more to spiritually prepare yourself and your sacred space. In doing so, you also prepare your mind and spirit to lead in the best way possible.

The most common way to cleanse your energy is to light a bundle of sage or a stick of Palo Santo wood and gently and intentionally wave the smoke around your body, starting with your head and working your way down to your toes. Then, intentionally smudge the smoke into every area of the space as you ask your guides for clearing. You can place the sage or wood in an abalone shell or another natural container, using a feather or your hand to fan the smoke. Work your way around the space, fanning the smoke into corners, windows, doorways, and all entry points. If indoors, open windows and doors to allow the old energy to leave.

As you wave the smoke around each area, say, "I release all energy that is stagnant or negative. All energy that is not in my highest and greatest good, please leave now. I clear this space to leave only room for peace, love, and joy."

Repeat this for all four corners of the space, and for each of the four directions, north, south, east and west. You may keep it simple as directed above, or you may recite the more in depth "opening sacred space" invocation process detailed in the next chapter.

An alternative to using sacred smoke is to use a spray such as a Palo Santo spray or your favorite essential oil. This works best when traveling or when in an area where smoke and fire is not safe to use.

Invoke your guides for assistance. Ask your guides, ancestors, and higher self to guide you in the ceremony to give the women the experience they need today.

You can ask for guidance by saying, "Please guide me to honor the women here today in the best possible way for their highest good with love and positive energy. Please help me provide a transformative healing experience to make their lives better. Thank you in advance."

Greet Your Tribe as They Arrive

As each woman arrives, greet them with a warm smile. Make each person feel welcome and loved. Giving a warm greeting is very important to the entire experience. Understand that some people who come may be a little hesitant about it; they may feel shy or uncomfortable. Your first most important job is to make them feel welcome, warm, and loved. Do this by hugging and saying to each one, "Thank you for coming. I'm so happy you're here."

Next, smudge each person with your sage, smudge stick, or spray. This will cleanse the energy of each person before they take their seat. Ask her to close her eyes (to protect from smoke or spray) and hold her arms straight out like a T. Begin by waving the smoke or spray starting at the head, working your way down and across her arms, then down to her toes. Ask her to turn around and repeat the process on her back side too.

While smudging her, say out loud, "We clear any energy you have been carrying that no longer serves you. We bring in a feeling of peace, love and joy. You are now cleared." Take deep breaths in between each sentence you speak. Put feeling into it as you smile and share your beautiful high energy.

Feel free to improvise and allow intuition to guide your words. For example, if you feel one of the ladies had a rough day, you may say, "We release all feelings of anxiety and stress from the day. We clear out any negative thoughts or acts that came your way today. We replace them with peace and joy. We now bring you the gentle vibrations of rest and relaxation. You are now cleared."

Hand each person the papers and pen they need for the journaling exercise.

Optional: You may offer other items, such as a candle they can light, a flower, a stone, or a crystal to hold.

At my ceremonies, I loan a crystal to each woman as they arrive. I keep an assortment of crystals in a box; amethyst, rose quartz, clear quartz, tourmaline, and many others. As each woman walks in, I hold out the box and invite them to choose one to hold during the ceremony.

My instructions are, "Pick up the first crystal that calls to you. Don't think about it; let your heart choose." The woman always chooses the stone she most needs for the evening. The crystal is held in the hand during the ceremony. At the end, the crystals are returned to the box. Later, I smudge the crystals to clear the energy so they are cleansed for the next ceremony.

The Ceremony

Your ceremony should have a beginning, middle, and closing. Know your intention for the ceremony in advance and how you will begin, execute, and close it. In this book I provide ready-to-go ceremonies. Trust your intuition and add your own personality, making any changes you feel will enhance the experience for your tribe. You can incorporate options such as sound healing, Reiki energy work, yoga, or any other mind-body-spirit practices.

The length of time for your ceremony may vary. Some ceremonies are only thirty minutes, others go for hours. The monthly ceremonies I hold are about 90 minutes long, including the sound healing session. Without sound healing my ceremonies are about 45 minutes or so. The ceremonies provided in each chapter will be about 30-60 minutes. You can choose how long you want your ceremony to be by following the chapter exactly, or you may want to add other activities which will make it longer.

Once everyone is seated, sound a bell or chime indicating it's time to start. The sound can be played with any instrument. In the absence of an instrument, get creative by tapping a glass with a spoon, ringing a bell, or hitting a drum.

Welcome your tribe and give an introduction to the ceremony. You may describe the intention for the ceremony and what they can expect. Always remind your tribe that anything shared is sacred and should be kept confidential, as this is a safe place for women to express themselves.

You may choose to include a talk about what the moon and cosmos are doing at that time. You might research the astrological update for that time period and share the information at the start of your ceremony. A good website with this information is www.Almanac.com or any astrologer's website you trust. You may also want to add a personal story or a reading from a book compatible with the theme and intention for the evening.

Follow the ceremony instructions in each section. Have fun with this; it's more enjoyable for all when you don't take it too seriously. Incorporate laughter wherever you can. Add a big sprinkle of love and understanding. Encourage everyone to open up and be comfortable.

Journaling

This portion of the ceremony is powerful because it guides the women to think, make decisions, and set intentions. When we write things down our intentions are recorded, not just physically on paper but imprinted in our minds. There is magic to writing down what you want and what you want to release.

Our journaling exercises are typically two parts; one is writing what you want to manifest or a gratitude list. These are things that you wish to keep; it's encouraged to keep this list where you will see it often. The second exercise is writing what you wish to release. At the end of the ceremony, you destroy the list of those items you want to release. This is done either by burning it safely, or putting it in a trash can.

The ceremonial process of writing what you want to call into your life and writing what you want to release invites the healing energies to come exactly when and where you need it.

Meditation

The guided meditations in this book are visualizations. They help shift your mind from everyday life and into yourself. Each meditation is designed for a specific purpose: a healing, manifestation, or a letting go.

Every single meditation in this book came to me from a higher power; it flowed into my consciousness as I wrote it out. Every month I prepare for my women's ceremony three days in advance. I meditate and ask a higher source for the words that will serve best. I learned over time to trust the process and allow the wisdom to flow through me.

The first few times I guided a meditation for a group of women, I was very nervous. I never really liked the sound of my raspy voice and I worried that my meditation wouldn't come across as authentic. I was afraid they wouldn't like it. But I also had a knowing that it was important to lead this way, so I pushed through my worries and did my best.

To my happy surprise, at nearly every ceremony, women would tell me how much my meditation helped them. After six months of guiding meditations, I finally stopped feeling nervous about it. I learned to trust myself.

If you feel nervous, one way to relax is realizing your meditation is not about you or about how you sound, it's about serving the women in the room. Focus on giving them the gift of the benefits meditation will bring to them. If you worry about how you sound, look, or deliver, ignore those worries and do your best. Do not try to be perfect. If you make a mistake while reading the meditation, chances are no one will notice.

You may want to play soft music in the background during meditation. Choose soothing music without lyrics. You can find suitable music from many online platforms such as YouTube and Spotify. Search for "meditation music" and "Reiki music" to find music that works best.

Begin the meditation by turning the lights down and inviting everyone to get very comfortable. For some that means lying down. For others it's sitting on a mat or in a chair. To signify the start of the meditation, sound a chime, bowl, or glass. Ask everyone to take a deep cleansing breath to relax into.

Read the meditation slowly. When guiding, it's important to take many long pauses. Speak softly, take a lot of deep breaths, and give the tribe a chance to get into their own quiet space.

Allow for frequent quiet pauses. There will be times when you should pause speaking for a minute or two. Frequent moments of silence allow time for their imaginations to work and get into their meditation zone. Use your intuition and feel free to change the wording in the meditations as needed. When meditation comes to a close, sound a chime, bowl, or glass to signify completion.

If you would like to listen to some of my recorded meditations for inspiration, or if you prefer to play a pre-recorded meditation for your tribe, you are welcome to access my videos of guided meditations online.

Go to my channel on YouTube.com by searching my name, Maria Brophy. There you'll find my playlist of recorded guided meditations.

Sharing and Holding Space

After each segment of the ceremony, you may want to ask if anyone wants to share their experience. You may want to set everyone at ease by sharing first.

Tell your tribe to quietly listen when someone is sharing. Sharing does not require a response; it's best to listen, acknowledge, and thank that person for sharing. This method of listening without giving opinions or answers is what we call "holding space." When someone is sharing you hold space for them by listening. There is no need to respond or try to solve their problem.

Some people may want to respond and give advice; note that your sharing segment may get out of hand if you have a tribe that likes to talk a lot! I've had circles where women start sharing and then others jump in with many talking over each other. I learned I had to take control and guide the circle to ensure an atmosphere of active listening and respect.

A great tool I like to use has been used for thousands of years by indigenous people: a talking stick. The talking stick is a wooden stick or staff handed to the person who will speak next. The bearer of the talking stick is the only one who can speak while the others listen quietly. When the speaker is finished, they offer the stick to the person who wants to speak next.

My talking stick was gifted to me; it's beautifully decorated with paint, ribbons, and a feather. You can make one by decorating a stick with paint and adding strips of fabric or feathers. Some add a rattle to the end so you can shake it when you want to punctuate a point you make.

Any stick will do; decorated or not, it will do the trick. If you don't have a stick, get creative and grab anything that can be passed around as a symbol of the talking stick.

Closing

Closing the ceremony is my favorite time, because everyone is very relaxed, sometimes laughing and sometimes crying. It reminds me of the slumber parties I enjoyed as a young girl. There is always a warm feeling of deep connection and togetherness.

At the end of your ceremony, you may close it by simply thanking every woman for being there. Remind them that the ceremony is a sacred, special time of healing and community. Encourage them to come again by announcing the date of the next one, inviting them to return then.

You may close out by offering to pull an oracle card, or by playing fun music to get everyone dancing. My full moon partner Christine sometimes hands out flowers saying, "You make the world a more beautiful place," to each woman as they leave.

Create your own special way of closing out your circle. Have fun with it. Enjoy knowing that you're helping to transform and heal the women in your community, which positively affects their families and radiates out into the world.

Cleanse Your Energy

Hosting a full moon ceremony requires a large output of energy from you. Sometimes the women who come have trauma and fears they leave behind. If not cleansed from you, it will stick, leaving you drained. This is why it's important to release and let go of anyone else's negative energies after a ceremony.

After everyone has left, cleanse your own energy and the energy of your space again with the smoke of burning sage or Palo Santo wood. You can also cleanse with a spray, or by taking an Epsom salt bath or shower. This clears out any energy that may have been picked up during the ceremony.

Close the sacred space by repeating the sacred space invocation again, as shown in the next chapter. You may choose to close sacred space in a simpler way by doing the following. Bring your hands together at your heart in prayer, then put them down by your sides. Then fan them up and out over your head, bringing your palms together again and down to your heart. Say, "Sacred space is now closed."

Thank your angels, guides, and your higher self for guiding you in the ceremony. Now you are complete.

CHAPTER 7
INVOCATION: OPENING SACRED SPACE PRAYER

Invocation: Opening Sacred Space

The following invocation/prayer is an option to create your sacred space before your tribe arrives. Another option is to recite and open sacred space in front of your people after they arrive and settle in. Do what feels best for you.

This invocation is often referred to as the "Four Winds." This prayer is generously shared on the website of Four Winds Society, a school of energy medicine and healing. To learn more about the origins of this invocation, go to: www.thefourwinds.com.

If you choose to use this invocation, it's important to use it with great respect and reverence. While reciting the invocation burn sage and wave it in every corner of the space. In between each direction, shake a rattle or hit a drum or bell four times.

Invocation

(Spoken facing south)

To the winds of the South:

Great Serpent,

Wrap your coils of light around us.

Teach us to shed the past the way you shed your skin,

To walk softly on the Earth.

Teach us the Beauty Way.

(Spoken facing west)

To the winds of the West:

Mother Jaguar,

Protect our medicine space.

Teach us the way of peace, to live impeccably.

Show us the way beyond death.

(Spoken facing north)

To the winds of the North:

Hummingbird, Grandmothers, and Grandfathers,

Ancient Ones.

Come and warm your hands by our fires.

Whisper to us in the wind.

We honor you who have come before us,

And you who will come after us, our children's children.

(Spoken facing east)

To the winds of the East:

Great Eagle, Condor,

Come to us from the place of the rising Sun.

Keep us under your wing.

Show us the mountains we only dare to dream of.

Teach us to fly wing to wing with the Great Spirit.

(Spoken with face down toward the ground)

Mother Earth:

We've gathered for the honoring of all your children,

The Stone People, the Plant People,

The four-legged, the two-legged, the creepy crawlers,

The finned, the furred, and the winged ones,

All our relations.

(Spoken with face up, toward the sky)

Father Sun, Grandmother Moon, to the Star Nations:

Great Spirit, you who are known by a thousand names

And you who are the unnamable One,

Thank you for bringing us together,

And allowing us to sing the Song of Life.

Sacred space is now open.

*Note: After your ceremony, close sacred space by repeating this process. At the end say, "Sacred space is now closed."

CHAPTER 8
JANUARY MOON: CLEAN THE SLATE

Full Moon Ceremony for the New Year

Intention: Identify goals and dreams you wish to cultivate in the new year. Clear out old energies, habits, and blocks to make room for new goals and dreams.

January offers a clean slate, a way to create a fresh new year for yourself. In this ceremony you make room for the new. Focus on creating a new reality through new feelings and new thoughts that deliver the life you want.

The mistake many people make after the new year is to push themselves to act on their new goals immediately. But January is a time to rest! It's a time to go within to reflect on what's worked in the past and identify what you need to change. It's a time to hibernate, journal, and take care of your emotional self.

January's moon offers an opportunity to make room for the new to come in. It prepares you for February, a perfect time to take action. January is a time to prime to take action right before the powerful energy of spring's emergence.

In this full moon ceremony, you will let go of blocks or stuck energy to make room for the new.

Set Your Sacred Space

Prepare your sacred space as directed in the "How to Use This Book" chapter.

Start by clearing your sacred space of any unwanted energy. Call in your guides and higher self to bring positive energy to the space.

Ask your guides, "Please provide me with the wisdom to create a powerful experience for the women who attend. Help me give them exactly what they need at this time. Allow me to be the light to raise their vibrations."

Welcome

Welcome your tribe into the space, one by one. Thank each person for coming. Make each one feel loved and special. Clear each woman's energy as she enters.

Invite her to find her space and get comfortable.

Opening

Open with a sound, chime, gong, or any audible indication that it's time to begin.

Ask everyone to become fully present. Help them settle in by asking them to take one deep breath in, hold it, and slowly release it completely.

Give a loving smile and tell your tribe what tonight's intention is and then begin the ceremony. Remind everyone that this is a safe space and anything shared in this circle is to be kept confidential.

Our intention is to release blocks and stuck energy to make room for your new year's choices.

In this ceremony you will:

1. **Choose** what you want to manifest for the new year.
2. **Release** blocks from the past that may hold you back.
3. **Inspire** your own action to lead to the manifestation of what you want.

Begin by telling a story about yourself or someone else that relates to the intention of this month's ceremony.

You may choose to pass the talking stick around the room and ask each woman to say their name and introduce themselves.

Another option, my favorite, is to ask each person to say their name and share one thing that everyone loves about them. This exercise is a beautiful way to help women embrace what is lovable about themselves by inviting them to look at themselves through the eyes of those who love them.

Journal Exercise

Make sure everyone has two small pieces of paper and a pen. Guide them through the exercise, allowing five minutes for each exercise.

Prepare for journaling by guiding everyone to close their eyes as they take one deep breath in and blow it out audibly (making a "whew" sound as they exhale). Then take another deep breath in and blow it out completely. Last, take a breath in and blow it out. This exercise helps you tap into your higher knowing for a better journaling experience.

Journal Exercise #1: Choose

Begin by making a list of things you wish to do this new year. Write down three things you intend to create. They can be material things, resolution of problems, relationships, new habits you wish to form, or anything you desire. (This paper will be reserved, kept as a reminder.) Now circle the one intention most important to you; you will commit to this one first.

Journal Exercise #2: Release Make room for the new things you intend to create by releasing thoughts, feelings and worries you have that may be holding you back. Write down three blocks that have kept you stuck from making your most important intention happen. These blocks can include thoughts and feelings such as:

- I am not good enough.
- I don't know how.
- A loved one wouldn't like it.
- I don't have time, money, or something else I need.
- I might fail.

Most of the things you think hold you back, don't actually hold you back —your belief in the thought holds you back. You can choose to release these blocks just by deciding to do it.

Now, write down the answer to this question: *Am I willing to release the energetic blocks holding me back?*

Tell your tribe it's okay if you're not ready to release a block. Sometimes you just aren't. You have to be honest with yourself. With honesty comes greater understanding. Some blocks are stubborn and feel too big to release. If so, hand it over to the Universe, your angels, or your guides to handle it for you.

If you're not ready to release those blocks, write down why. (This paper will be burned or destroyed at the end of the ceremony.)

. . .

Meditation

Note to reader: Take long pauses in between each visualization segment. Moments of silence will allow your tribe to better ease into the meditation.

Get your body settled into a comfortable position.

Close your eyes.

Feel your eyes relax.

Relax your jaw.

Feel the jaw muscles release.

Relax your body.

Take a deep cleansing breath in.

Hold for one, two, three.

Release the breath as you release tension from the day.

Place one hand on your heart space, that little spot located in between your breasts. This calms your nervous system.

Take another deep breath in. Feel as your breath fills your heart space. Blow the breath out of your mouth.

One more deep breath in.

Hold for one, two, three.

Audibly blow the breath out, *ahhh.*

The full moon is glowing above this space, high in the sky.

. . .

Visualize the moon's bright light shining on the top of your head. Feel its cleansing energy on your crown.

Breathe into it for three breaths, as you continue to focus on the moon's light shining on your crown.

Reader, *pause for a minute.*

Now, think for a moment of that one nagging worry that's been on your mind, a worry that you have been harboring.

Ask the moon, in your mind, "Please wash this worry away from me right now."

Take a deep breath in and out.

See the golden glow of the moonlight wash over your head and clear your mind.

Feel it cleanse and release your worry.

Trust as you let it go.

Breathe in and out.

Watch the worry float away into the night sky, and then see it dissipate into nothingness.

Enjoy a feeling of relief and renewal.

Now, visualize and feel the cleansing moonlight seep and flow down into your heart space.

Within your heart is a sadness, a disappointment, that has taken up space there.

Feel into that sadness for a moment. Allow it to speak to you.

Allow the feeling of it.

Notice how this sad feeling affects your physical heart space.

Reader: Pause for a few minutes to allow them to feel into the meditation.

Now, breathe in the moon's golden light.

Visualize the light expanding your heart space, filling it with cleansing loving forgiving light.

Take a deep breath in. As you exhale, release the sadness to the sky.

Now, feel your newly cleansed heart space. Feel how much space is there now. Allow more love into the space you just cleared.

Sit in the feeling that you are love.

Sit in the feeling that you have love inside you.

Sit in the feeling that you are loved.

Now … visualize the golden moonlight flowing down your body to the base of your spine. This is your root chakra. It regulates your feeling of security and safety.

There is a tiny fear residing there. A fear that you have been harboring. Identify what that fear is. Your first thought is the right one.

Reader: Pause a few minutes.

Offer that fear compassion, as if it were a lost child.

Feel into the fear for a moment. Allow it to express itself.

And now thank it for wanting to protect you.

Now say to that fear, in your mind, "I release you to the Universe."

"I ask my guides to transmute you into love."

Take in a deep breath. As you release, see your fear float out of your body and up into the sky. Watch as it disappears.

Feel the feeling that you are safe. You are protected. You are okay, always.

Reader: Pause for a minute.

Now, visualize the moon's golden light as it illuminates your body from the crown of your head all the way down to your toes.

Feel refreshed and renewed.

Take one last breath in.

Release it.

Take a few minutes to enjoy the feeling of your cleared energy.

Open your eyes, we are complete.

Take your time getting up.

Sharing

If you desire, pass a talking stick around the circle and hand it to anyone who wants to share their thoughts, feelings, fears, and experiences with journaling and/or meditation.

Encourage sharing by taking the first turn. Tell your tribe your own journaling answers, or a story about overcoming a fear to act on something you'd been wanting to do. Sharing can be the most impactful part of the circle, as it encourages introspection, connection, and compassion.

. . .

Burn/Destroy Your Release Paper

Guide your tribe to destroy the journal exercise #2 paper, including the items they wish to release. This can be done either by safely burning the paper, or by tearing it up and throwing it in the trash.

Before destroying the paper tell yourself, "I now release these things I no longer wish to hold onto."

Closing

Close the gathering by guiding everyone in a simple prayer of gratitude. You may want to invite everyone to hold hands for added connection.

"We are grateful for this time of healing. We appreciate the love and open minds of the women here right now. We commit to spreading this beautiful energy into the world when we leave this ceremony today. Close your eyes and smile as you think of one thing you're personally grateful for right now."

Thank everyone for coming. Tell them to take their time as they gather their things.

Remember to close your sacred space at the very end. You may do this by simply saying, "Sacred space is now closed," or by reciting the Four Winds invocation offered in a previous section of this book.

Extra Special

You may add to the experience by inviting your tribe to pull an oracle card before leaving.

You may also add a special group prayer for someone in need, or for someone who is ill or suffering. Or you may say a group prayer for the world.

Gift each person a crystal, stone, or essential oil, anything that may be symbolic of the work done in the ceremony.

Play energizing, uplifting music as people gather their things and prepare to leave. Invite everyone to do a fun dance to music before they leave.

Use your imagination and creativity to add your own personality to this ceremony. Trust your ideas, as they come from a higher source.

CHAPTER 9
FEBRUARY MOON: CRITICISM AND CREATIVITY

Full Moon Ceremony to Bypass Criticism and Allow Creative Expression

Intention: This ceremony is meant to encourage you to bypass criticism and allow yourself to express your creativity and give life to the burning desire you've been hiding.

Everyone has creativity inside them; it's not just for poets and painters. Mothers are creative with their babies' birthday celebrations, entrepreneurs are creative when setting up their businesses, you are creative when you express yourself on social media.

Too often, creativity is stifled due to fear of criticism. Society, parents, and well-meaning teachers in our lives have made us feel as though our ideas are not valid.

Fear of criticism can silence. Silence creates stagnation. Stagnation leads to unhappiness and illness.

When you feel a burning desire to express yourself in any way, let it out despite what others might say. The burning desire comes from a higher place, and you must not stifle it.

When you stifle your ideas, you're not able to live your best life. Many of you will dream of those things you'd love to do, yet you never take action on it. You have this idea that you'll do it later when circumstances are better.

The problem is that later never comes. You have to make space for it now, while you can. Making space means you intentionally set up your months, weeks, and days for it. You have to do it regardless of anyone else's opinion.

Before you intentionally set aside time to do that which you love, you have to identify the things you want to do.

Many of us lose sight of our burning desires. Often your burning desires were with you as a child, but you were told by well-meaning adults to stop dreaming about them. Over time you completely forgot what you dreamed of, and you replaced it with the dreams of others.

When I was a teenager, I knew I wanted to be an author, but I didn't believe in myself enough to take steps toward it. My creative block was I wasn't good enough, that I didn't know enough, and that people who grew up poor like me didn't get opportunities like that.

It wasn't until I was in my forties that I learned I could express myself through writing without someone else's approval. One day I felt so sick and tired of not expressing myself I decided I would write every single morning when I woke up. At first it was just musings and jumbled writings that didn't add up to much. Eventually, though, my daily practice evolved into writing a book for artists, teaching them how to sell art, as that is my talent in business. A few years later, I published my first book titled, *Art Money Success,* and it became an Amazon best seller.

I spent the first half of my life stunting my creative energies because I was afraid to express myself. Now well into my fifties, I'm expressing myself in my own way. I'm finding out that while some of my family may not agree with what I'm doing, many others are inspired by it.

This ceremony will unveil your burning desires and inspire you to allow your creativity to flow.

Set Your Sacred Space

Prepare your sacred space as directed in the "How to Use This Book" chapter.

Clear your sacred space of any unwanted energy, and call in your guides and higher self to bring positive energy to the space. Ask your guides, "Please flow wisdom through me so I may give great inspiration to the women who come. Help me give them exactly what they need at this time, and allow me to be the light to raise their vibrations."

Welcome

Welcome your tribe into the space, one by one. Thank each person for being here. Make each person feel loved and accepted. Clear each woman's energy as she enters. Invite her to find her space and get comfortable.

Opening

Open with a sound, chime, gong, or any audible indication that it's time to begin.

Ask everyone to become fully present. Help them settle in by asking them to take one deep breath in, hold it, and slowly release it completely.

Give a loving smile and tell your tribe about tonight's intention, then begin the ceremony. Remind everyone that this is a safe space and anything shared in this circle is to be kept confidential.

You may choose to pass the talking stick around the room and ask each woman to say their name and introduce themselves. Another option, one of my favorites, is to ask each person to say their name and share one thing that everyone loves about them. This exercise is a beautiful way to help women embrace something lovable about themselves by inviting them to look at themselves through the eyes of those who love them.

In this ceremony you will:

1. **Identify** what you would love to express.
2. **Release** that which holds you back.

3. **Inspire** you to put it into daily practice.

Journal Exercise

Make sure everyone has two pieces of paper and a pen. Guide them through this exercise, allowing five minutes for each. Use a timer set to five minutes. After you give instructions for each exercise, have a few minutes of silence to allow the women to go deep within as they write.

Prepare for journaling by guiding everyone to close their eyes as they take one deep breath in and blow it out audibly, making a "whew" sound as they blow it out. Then take another deep breath in and blow it out completely. Lastly, take a third breath in and blow it out. This breathing exercise invites your higher knowing for a better journaling experience.

Journaling exercise #1: Identify In this exercise, instruct your tribe to keep writing until the five-minute timer goes off. Do not put your pen down until the timer goes off. Do not stop writing until the timer goes off. Instruct them that if they run out of things to write, they should make things up. This will pull from the deep recesses of your mind. This process can be magical!

We begin by making a list of burning desires. Write a long list of things you would LOVE to do or have. This can include places you want to go, things you want to create, things you want to become, relationship goals, etc.

Maintain silence for five minutes. (This paper will be reserved and kept as a reminder.) If you see someone put their pen down, remind the tribe to keep writing until the timer goes off.

After the timer sounds, instruct everyone to circle the top three things they would love, paying special attention to the desires they wrote down they've been carrying since childhood.

Journaling exercise #2: Release In this exercise, instruct your tribe to write a list of people, reasons, and things that held them back from the desires they wrote on the first page. Set the timer for five minutes, and remind them again to keep writing, and don't put the pen down, even if it means they have to make things up.

After the timer goes off, instruct everyone to write at the bottom of the paper, "Should this really hold me back?" Then answer the question.

(The paper will be burned or destroyed at the end of the ceremony.)

Meditation: Into the Rainbow Tunnel

Note to reader: Take long pauses in between each visualization segment. Moments of silence allow your tribe to better ease into the meditation.

Today's meditation will unveil your longing or discontent and will allow your creative energy to show itself.

Get into a comfortable position. You may sit up or lie down, whichever allows you to go deep within.

Close your eyes.

Relax your body. Feel the worries of the day fall away as you breath in and out.

Begin by grounding yourself.

Take a deep cleansing breath in.

Hold for a count of three.

One, two, three.

Release any tension you picked up throughout the day as you release your breath out.

Now imagine in your mind's eye that there are thick, healthy roots growing out of the soles of your feet and spine. Visualize these three roots traveling deep into the ground, all the way down into the center of the earth.

In the earth's center is a large crystal cave, and in the center of the cave there's a large clear quartz crystal, shimmering brightly. See your roots wrap around the crystal three times.

One.

Two.

Three.

Now imagine the crystal is sending high-vibration energy up through your roots, through the soles of your feet and spine, up through your body and out the top of your head. Notice how good that feels.

Now, place one hand on your belly. Breathe in and feel your belly rise. Breathe out and feel your belly fall.

Breathe in.

Breathe out.

Breathe in.

Breathe out.

Note to reader: *Pause for a minute.*

Visualize a golden ball of light a few inches above your head. See it shower you with light and fill your entire body with golden light. Watch as the light forms a protective bubble around your body. This is your protection.

Now visualize yourself walking on a beach, barefoot in the sand. Feel the sand beneath your feet, the sun on your face. Hear the waves lap on the shore. See yourself smile as you bask in joy.

As you walk on the sand, invite a thought to pop into your head. Think of one thing you've been holding tight in your heart, one strong desire you've wanted to express in a certain way, but you've been holding back. Hold that desire in your mind for a moment.

Continue walking in the sand and see a beautiful rainbow up ahead, stretched across the beach like a tunnel. The colors are intense, and you feel a strong connection to it. You walk up to the rainbow and enter it, instantly feeling love and acceptance. Notice what that feels like. This is a safe place. In this rainbow tunnel, you are deeply loved for one reason only, not because of who you are. You are loved because *you are.*

You were born loved just because you are. Feel what that feels like.

Note to reader: *Pause for a minute.*

Now, look ahead deeper into the rainbow tunnel and keep walking through it. Up ahead you see a beautiful creature waiting for you. She glows, and you can feel her love and curiosity for you. This creature safeguards all the secrets of the Universe.

She beckons you to come closer. As you walk closer, you feel her love and acceptance get stronger and stronger. The creature has a question for you: when you hear her question, answer in your mind with the first thought that pops into your head.

The creature asks: "Tell me the one burning thing you desire to express." It's safe to tell her; give her your answer right now.

Note to reader: Pause for a minute.

Allow your words to swirl around her as she listens with complete love and acceptance. Notice how it feels to be heard. *Know* you are always safe to express yourself.

Now, hug the magical creature goodbye. Feel her encouragement as she hugs you with a knowing that you're on your right path. She gives you a shining star that fits in the palm of your hand; the star represents courage. Close your hand and hold the star as it fills you with its essence of courage to shine your light.

Turn around and walk through the rainbow back to its opening. Now step back on the sand and look at the ocean.

Bring your feeling of courage to express yourself back into your life here and now. Feel the star warm your hand as it slowly disappears, leaving you with the courage you need.

Note to reader: Pause for a minute.

Let's seal this practice with one last deep breath in and out. Breathe in. Breathe out. Open your eyes.

We are complete.

Sharing

If you desire, pass a talking stick around the circle and hand it to anyone who wants to share their thoughts, feelings, fears, or experience with journaling and meditation.

Remind everyone that whatever is shared in the circle is to be kept confidential and private. Encourage sharing by taking the first turn if you have something you wish to share.

Burn/Destroy Your Release Paper

Guide your tribe to destroy the journal exercise #2 paper, including those items they wish to release. This can be done either by safely burning the paper, or by tearing it up and throwing it in a trash can. Before destroying it, tell yourself, "I now release these blocks I no longer wish to hold onto."

Closing

Close the gathering by guiding everyone in a simple prayer of gratitude. You may want to invite everyone to hold hands for added connection. Say something along these lines:

"We are grateful for this time of growth. We appreciate the love and open minds of the women here right now. We commit to spreading this beautiful energy out into the world when we leave the ceremony today. Let's all close our eyes and smile as you think of one thing you're personally grateful for right now."

Thank everyone for coming. Tell them to take their time as they gather their things.

Remember to close your sacred space at the very end. You may do this by simply saying, "Sacred space is now closed," or by reciting the Four Winds invocation offered in a previous section of this book. Be sure to cleanse your own energy after everyone leaves.

Extra Special

You may add a special group prayer for someone in need, or for someone who is ill or suffering. Or you may say a group prayer for the world.

Before leaving, invite your tribe to pull an oracle card. You can also gift each person a crystal, stone, essential oil, or anything that may be symbolic of the work done in this ceremony.

Play uplifting energizing music as people gather their things and prepare to leave.

Use your imagination and creativity to add your own personality to the ceremony. Trust your ideas, as they come from a higher source.

CHAPTER 10
MARCH MOON: SPRING EQUINOX

Full Moon During Spring Equinox

Intention: Our intention is to plant the seeds for what we wish to manifest as we celebrate moving away from the dark days of winter and into the sunshine of spring. You will plant seeds for what you intend to grow in this new season.

In March we embrace the energy of the spring equinox. Spring equinox typically falls around March 20th. Try to schedule your ceremony date on a full moon as close to that date as possible.

This ceremony can be very powerful for manifesting. The first time my Sisters of the Moon companions and I hosted a spring equinox ceremony it was March 2022. A woman named Lori came to our event; she was new to town and in a huge life transition phase. She had been divorced for two years and still was trying to find her way. She was shy on arrival and limping. She had broken her knee and her mother had died just two weeks prior. She was broken both spiritually and physically. She was living temporarily with her cousin, confused about what to do with her life. She didn't know anyone in town and was looking for a place to live. Everything in her life was upside down.

The journaling exercise helped her get clear about what she wanted. She wrote that she wanted, "A cheap place to live at the beach. A part time job. A new life."

We led the women in an eye-gazing experience, which is detailed below and should be experienced before the guided meditation.

During the eye-gazing part of our ceremony, miraculous things happened! Lori's eye-gazing partner, Barb, felt and transferred the presence of Lori's mother. Lori and Barb, having never met before, connected deeply on a spiritual level. The exchange between them helped Lori release some of her bottled-up feelings and prepped her for the meditation that followed. Tears flowed through most of the evening as Lori released fears and past hurts.

Her manifestation came quickly. Two days after our ceremony, Lori's cousin gave her one week to move out. This was the catalyst for getting what she dreamed of. Lori told a few people she was looking for a room to rent, and very quickly and easily the Universe delivered one to her. When Lori was at the grocery store she ran into someone who heard she was looking. The new acquaintance said, "I know a lady who has a large house at the beach and needs someone to help her with her two broken arms." The Universe brought her the right people to bring her dreams to life. Not only did Lori find a low-cost place to live, but a part-time job as well. Her new life at the beach had begun.

The spring equinox practice can bring together what you need to manifest the things you dream of.

Set Your Sacred Space

Set up your space and add symbolic equinox items such as seeds, a spring flower, or an egg. Clear your sacred space of unwanted energy. Call in your guides and higher self to bring positive energy to the space.

Ask your guides, "Please provide me with the wisdom to create a powerful experience for the women who attend. Help me give them exactly what they need at this time. Allow me to be the light to raise their vibrations."

Welcome

Welcome your tribe into the space, one by one. Thank each person for being here. Make every single one of them feel loved and welcome. Clear each woman's energy as she enters. Invite her to find her space and get comfortable.

Opening

Open with a sound, chime, gong, or any audible indication that it's time to begin.

Ask everyone to become fully present. Help them settle in by asking them to take one deep breath in, hold it, and slowly release it completely.

You may choose to begin by guiding everyone to chant Om together. Ask them to take a deep breath and on the exhale start the Om chant by making the long O sound, followed by the M sound. Encourage your tribe to repeat the chant three times together, allowing the sound to resonate and vibrate within them. After the third Om chant, sit in stillness for a moment to absorb the effects of the practice. Ask them to notice any shifts in their body, mind, and energy. (Note: you can find an Om chant on YouTube to listen to as a guide for the chants if that makes it easier for you. Or first practice this alone before the ceremony.)

Give a loving smile and tell your tribe what tonight's intention is, then begin the ceremony. Remind everyone that this is a safe space and anything shared in the circle is to be kept confidential.

The spring equinox is the time when winter moves into spring and daylight hours are equal to nighttime hours. During this time, the veil between the physical world and the spiritual world is thinner. This opens us to receive more insights, as our intuition is stronger. When we gather women together in ceremony during this time we create a catalyst for healing, insight, and breakthroughs. It's a powerful time to set new intentions we want to bring to life in the spring season.

To help us manifest our new intentions, we first have to prepare ourselves. This ceremony will guide you through the process.

Just like when you grow a garden, you first must choose the seeds of the plants you intend to grow. You must prepare the soil and then you can create a vibration that will pull in all the resources needed to nourish your plants.

In this ceremony we will:

1. **Choose the seeds** to nourish and grow (your goals and desires).
2. **Prepare the soil** by removing weeds (the things that hold you back).
3. **Set intentions** and give life to the dream so you can attract the people and things to help you nourish and grow your garden.

Dreams often require resources and the help of others. When you're free of blocks and open to receiving, those resources come easily, just like the sun and the rain. But sometimes you unknowingly have invisible walls that block you from attracting the people and resources you need. As soon as you remove those blocks, you're free to attract all the people and resources required to make your dream come to life.

Journal Exercise

Make sure everyone has two small pieces of paper and a pen. Guide them through this exercise, allowing five minutes for each step.

Prepare for journaling by guiding everyone to close their eyes as they take one deep breath in and blow it out audibly by making a "whew" sound as they blow out. Then take another deep breath in and blow it out completely. Lastly, take a breath in and blow it out. This breathing exercise helps tap into your higher knowing for a better journaling experience.

Journaling Exercise #1: Creation Begin by making a list of seeds you wish to plant and grow this season. Write down five things you desire and intend to create this spring. It can be material things, resolution of problems, something you want to create, relationships, new habits you wish to form, anything you desire. (This paper will be reserved and kept as a reminder.) Circle the one intention that is most important to you.

Journaling exercise #2: Release Prepare the soil by writing three things that may have been holding you back from making your most important intention happen. Then write this question, "Am I willing to release the things that hold me back?" Then answer the question. (This paper will be burned or destroyed at the end of the ceremony.)

Eye Gazing

This is an optional exercise, but one that I highly recommend adding for the spring equinox gathering. It helps prepare the soil for planting seeds by removing the "weeds" in your mind. Usually, when you think about what holds you back from achieving your goals, we blame lack of time, lack of knowledge, lack of resources. But we miss the fact that you've unconsciously created an invisible shield. The invisible shield comes from past disappointments and hurts. It is designed to protect you from others.

One easy way to break down invisible shields is through eye gazing. This brings you deeply in touch with the power of the Universe, the power that pulls all resources to you when you need them. Start with two people sitting close to each other staring into each other's eyes for ten minutes or longer.

Wild things can happen during eye gazing. First, people giggle. Then they try hard to focus. After a few minutes, deep connection begins to form. Some people cry as they realize that "I am you and you are me." It's amazing to watch as barriers dissolve.

I must warn you that this exercise is hard for some people. It can be uncomfortable and you may get resistance from your tribe. But they will thank you later because it will create a profound transformation they'll never forget.

First, pair each participant with a partner. If you have an uneven number of guests, you as the guide will sit out, which is okay because as facilitator you can watch the reactions of your participants. When choosing partners, allow the process to happen organically without direction.

Give your tribe the following instructions:

- Sit as close to your partner as comfortable, eye to eye.
- Stare into her eyes and maintain your gaze until the timer sounds.
- Do not speak during this time.
- Go with the flow; allow all feelings to surface.
- Laugh if you must; cry if you must.
- Don't drop your gaze or look away until the timer sounds.

It's okay to laugh, cry, and feel strong emotions. Allow feelings to bubble up.

See beyond the eyes, feel who your partner really is, and see yourself in her eyes.

Give her acceptance and feel her acceptance of you.

Now, set the timer for ten minutes of silence. When the timer goes off, thank your partner and suggest a hug. Ask if anyone wants to share and pass the talking stick to allow sharing.

Tell them, "You have prepared the soil. Now it's time to plant your seeds." Then guide the meditation below.

Spring Equinox Meditation

Get into a comfortable position, either seated or lying down. Close your eyes and settle in. Take a deep cleansing breath in. Let it out nice and slow.

Visualize yourself standing in a grassy meadow. The sun is shining brightly overhead. You are barefoot and your feet sink into the soft grass. Imagine a thick root growing from the bottom of each foot, burrowing deep into the earth and anchoring you to the ground.

Visualize the roots traveling deep into the center of the earth to a large clear quartz crystal. Watch as your roots wrap around the crystal three times.

One.

Two.

Three.

Feel the crystal energy traveling up through the roots to the surface of the earth and back into the bottom of your feet. Allow energy to travel gently up your legs, up your spine, and out the top of your head. You are now grounded.

Imagine the sun as a bright, glowing ball of light high above your head. See its beautiful life-giving energy shine on the top of your head.

See the sunshine rain on the crown of your head, showering down as it lights your throat chakra, heart space, solar plexus, through your uterus and out the base of your spine. Allow the bright sunshine to light up your entire body. See yourself glowing with this light. Take a deep breath in and out.

Visualize yourself looking over the beautiful meadow you're standing in. Notice a clearing of fresh soil ready for planting. Beside the fresh soil is a burlap bag full of seeds. See your name on the burlap bag with the word *Dreams* written on it. This bag contains all your dreams, desires, and goals.

Reach into the bag and choose one goal you wish to grow and nurture right now. Pull a seed out of the bag and kneel to lovingly place it into the soil. Gently cover your seed with dirt.

Now, look up to the sky and ask the heavens to rain on your seed. Watch as the rain moistens the soil.

Note to reader: *Pause here for a minute.*

See your seed grow into a small, green seedling shooting out of the soil. Look into the sky again and ask the sun to shine on the seedling and watch as its strong rays illuminate your seedling, making it grow taller.

Enjoy the unfolding process. Feel the satisfaction of watching the Universe bring all necessary nourishment to grow your seed. Now, step away from your seedling and look to the north. Take a moment to imagine what your real-life goal will look like when it's manifested.

Note to reader: *Pause here for a minute.*

Imagine how you will **feel** and who it will **impact.** Visualize what you'll be doing when this goal comes to life.

Note to reader: Pause here for two minutes.

Walk closer to your seedling and ask the sun to keep it warm and the sky to nourish it. Tell your seedling, "I love you. I nurture you. I will enjoy the process of watching you grow. I allow the Universe to bring all the nourishment needed to bring you to life."

Now, put a smile on your face. Look up and thank the sun and the sky for helping you grow. They represent all the people in the Universe who will come to your aid to help manifest your goal.

Take one final deep breath in and out. Open your eyes; we are complete.

Burn/Destroy Your Release Paper

Guide your tribe to destroy the paper for this journal exercise, including the items they wish to release. This can be done either by safely burning the paper in a fire, or by tearing it up and throwing it in a trash can. Before destroying it, tell yourself, "I now release these things I no longer wish to hold onto."

Closing

Close the gathering by guiding everyone to hold hands and lead a simple prayer of gratitude.

"We are grateful for this time of growth. We appreciate the love and open minds of the women here now. We commit to bringing this beautiful energy into the world when we leave this ceremony today. Close your eyes and smile as you think of one thing that you're grateful for right now."

Thank everyone for coming. Tell them to take their time as they gather their things.

Remember to close your sacred space at the very end. You may do this by simply saying, "Sacred space now closed," or by reciting the Four Winds invocation offered in a previous section of this book.

Make sure you smudge yourself after everyone leaves to clear unwanted energy that may have attached to you during the ceremony.

Extra Special

You may add a special group prayer for someone in need, or for someone who is ill or suffering, or you may say a group prayer for the world. Invite participants to pull an oracle card before leaving. You may decide to gift each person a seedling, flower, or anything else symbolic of the work done in this circle.

Play uplifting energizing music as people gather their things and prepare to leave.

Use your imagination and creativity to add your own personality to the ceremony. Trust your ideas, as they come from a higher source.

CHAPTER 11
APRIL MOON: EGYPTIAN ACTIVATION OF INTUITION

*I*ntention: *In this full moon ceremony we will activate and strengthen our intuition, accessing the wisdom from ancient Egypt.*

There was a time in history many thousands of years ago when women ruled the earth. Their intuition and ability to give life made them all-powerful. Men provided physical protection for their female goddesses, allowing them to focus their energies on healing, love, and community. The symbiotic relationship between the masculine and the feminine was harmonious. This knowledge was suppressed for centuries and is now being uncovered by researchers.

A woman's intuition is always accurate. Think of a time a warning light flashed in your mind telling you to beware of a person or a situation. It was likely right every single time.

This inner knowing, your intuition, is your birthright. It's a powerful feature that women innately possess to help them navigate life more easily. The problem is that many of us were taught to distrust our inner knowing. We've been trained to look outside ourselves for wisdom. Most of us have lost trust in our abilities. Over time, we might even have gotten in the habit of confusing our misguided fearful thoughts with intuition.

When you intentionally use your intuition, it gets stronger. As it strengthens, you learn how to discern between true intuition (which is always accurate) and your monkey mind thoughts (which is often inaccurate).

As your intuition gets stronger, you learn to trust it more and more. You will not need to seek answers from others, as you will know you can access all answers by getting quiet and listening to your higher self.

This ceremony will kickstart your intuitive powers. In the meditation for this ceremony, we will visit the Great Pyramid of Egypt in our minds and tap into the energy of intuition by connecting with the ancient wisdom residing in the pyramid stones. Visualization will activate your intuitive powers and you'll have greater ability to tap into inner wisdom you may not have been aware of.

If you knew how much power you possess inside yourself, you would never again be afraid, lonely, or unsure. You can use your intuition to guide decisions so your actions are in the highest good for all.

Set Your Sacred Space

Prepare your sacred space as directed in the chapter, "How to Use This Book."

Clear your sacred space of any unwanted energy. You may want to add symbols from Egypt to your alter: the all-seeing eye, pyramids, an ankh, or anything else symbolic of ancient Egyptian wisdom.

Call in your guides and higher self to bring positive energy to the intended space.

Ask your guides, "Please flow wisdom through me so I may give great inspiration to the women who come. Help me tap into my innate wisdom. Allow me to be the light and raise their vibrations as I encourage them to trust their own inner wisdom."

Welcome

Welcome your tribe into the space, one by one. Thank each person for attending. Make each one feel warmly loved and important. Clear each woman's energy as she enters. Invite her to find her space and get comfortable.

Opening

Open with a sound, chime, gong, or any audible indication that it's time to begin.

Ask everyone to become fully present. Help them settle in by taking one deep breath in, hold it, and slowly release it completely.

Give a loving smile and tell your tribe what tonight's intention is and begin the ceremony. Remind everyone this is a safe space and that anything shared in the circle is to be kept confidential.

You may choose to pass the talking stick around the room and ask each woman to say their name and introduce themselves. You may choose to ask each person to say their name and share one thing everyone loves about them. This exercise is a beautiful way to help women embrace what is lovable about themselves by inviting them to look at themselves through the eyes of those who love them.

You may also begin a conversation about intuition and share a story about a time you tapped into your intuition for guidance or tell a story someone else has shared online or with you in the past.

Intention: Our intention is to recognize the power of intuition. We will activate and strengthen it.

In this ceremony we will:

1. **Choose** the number one area of your life where you want to use your intuition for guidance.
2. **Release** the number one reason you haven't fully trusted your intuition in the past.
3. **Visit** ancient Egypt in a meditation to help you identify one past event that held you back, then dissolve it.

Journal Exercise

Make sure everyone has two small pieces of paper and a pen. Guide them through this exercise, allowing five minutes of silence for each step.

Prepare for journaling by guiding everyone to close their eyes as they take one deep breath in and blow it out audibly (making a "whew" sound as they blow it out). Then take another deep breath in and blow it out completely. Lastly, take a breath in and blow it out. This breathing exercise helps you tap into your higher knowing for a better journaling experience.

Journaling Exercise #1: Choose Begin by writing a list of the areas of your life for which you're seeking answers. Example: How to improve a relationship, how to deal with your children, how to find your dream job, how to get your body in shape, how to solve a current life problem, etc. (This paper will be reserved and kept as a reminder.)

Now circle the one area in your life that is most important to you to find answers.

Journaling Exercise #2: Release Answer this question, "Why do I not fully trust myself to find answers within?" Write anything that comes to mind. Do a brain dump and let it out. Example: "I don't know how, I made mistakes before, I've been told this is the way it is, etc." (This paper will be burned or destroyed at the end of the ceremony.)

Now guide your tribe to circle the one answer that stands out to you the most true.

Meditation: Exploring Ancient Egypt

In this guided visualization we will journey to ancient Egypt. Get in a comfortable position lying down or sitting up.

Close your eyes.

Take a deep breath in and hold it for three seconds. Release it completely.

Take another deep breath in and hold it for three seconds.

As you release, pull your belly button toward your spine so you empty it completely.

Let's do that again.

Take a deep breath in.

Hold the breath for one, two, three.

Release it completely.

Now breathe normally and notice your belly rising and falling with each breath.

Now we will ground ourselves by putting roots into Mother Earth.

Visualize thick healthy roots growing from the soles of your feet. Watch as the roots dig into the floor and travel deep to the center of the earth. There you see a large clear quartz crystal in the center of a giant cavern. Intentionally wrap your roots around the crystal three times.

One.

Two.

Three.

This will keep you grounded as you travel to Egypt, an ancient civilization that revered the power of the feminine.

Visualize your body as a white light, floating above the ground and up to the sky. See yourself flying across the world, all the way to the other side of the planet, to the Giza Plateau in Egypt.

As you approach the Giza plateau, notice three enormous pyramids below you. The middle pyramid is the tallest, the Great Pyramid.

Float to the opening of the Great Pyramid. Take a close look at the giant granite stones that make up the pyramid.

Ancient wisdom has been held in these stones for hundreds of thousands of years. Place your hands flat against the stones and feel the energy coming from them.

Now, visualize yourself floating into the entrance of the pyramid and traveling through the long, narrow tunnel that takes you inside. It's dark and cool inside. You can feel the healing energy sealed inside the stones.

See yourself float to the end of the tunnel and out the end of it. You are now in a large open room, the King's Chambers, which is 35 feet long. Its walls are made of pink granite stones. The stones contain beautiful, powerful spiritual energy from ancient times.

There's only one thing inside the King's Chamber, located in the back of the room: a large black granite box. Take a moment to feel the ancient energy of this space—it is loving, powerful, and all-knowing. Soak in the ancient power of this pyramid.

Note to reader: Pause here for two minutes.

Now, look beyond the granite box. There is something moving playfully behind it in the shadows. Look closer and see a cute little girl hiding from you. Walk over to her and look at her closely. See her face. Notice what she' wearing. Notice her hair and every detail about this little girl. Feel into the essence of who she is.

Realize that this little girl is *you* as a child.

Note to reader: Pause here for two minutes.

Now, tap into the girl's thoughts. Ask her, "When did you learn to believe you were less than perfect?" Listen to her answer and trust that it is true.

Note to reader: Pause here for two minutes.

Now, walk over and hug your little girl. Tap into the wisdom you have now as a grown woman and transfer it to her. Hug her tighter as you give her your love. Feel the love as you give it to her.

Tell this little girl all the good things that will happen in her life as she grows up. List all the great people you've brought into your life, all the fun things you've done, all the good things that came to you.

Note to reader: Pause here for two minutes.

Now, look at your little girl and tell her, "You are powerful. You are loved. You are worthy of all-that-is." Look in her eyes and see that she understands and believes you. Take a moment to stay in the feeling of powerful love and understanding.

Note to reader: Pause here for a minute.

Now, tuck that little girl under your arm and float her up and out of the pyramid, through the sky, around the earth and back home with you. Bring her into this space here and now and allow her to be a part of this practice.

You just changed your past for a better future. Let's all take a deep breath in to seal this practice. Release the breath.

And we are complete. Open your eyes when you are ready.

Burn/Destroy Your Release Paper

Guide your tribe to destroy the journal exercise #2 paper, including the items they wish to release. This can be done either by safely burning the paper, or by tearing it up and throwing it in a trash can. Before destroying it tell yourself, "I now release these things that have held me back from fully trusting myself."

Closing the Sacred Circle

Close the circle by guiding everyone to hold hands and lead a simple prayer of gratitude:

"We are grateful for this time of healing. We appreciate the love and open minds of the women here right now. We commit to bringing this beautiful energy into the world when we leave the ceremony today. Close your eyes and smile as you think of one thing you're grateful for right now."

Thank everyone for coming. Tell them to take their time as they gather their things.

Remember to close your sacred space at the very end. You may do this by simply saying, "Sacred space now closed," or by reciting the Four Winds invocation offered in an earlier section of this book.

Be sure to smudge yourself completely after everyone leaves, to release any unwanted energies that may have attached to you during the ceremony.

Extra Special

You may add a special group prayer for someone in need, or for someone who is ill or suffering. You may also say a group prayer for the world.

You can add to the experience by handing each person a trinket or symbol of ancient Egyptian wisdom to take home with them. You can also invite them to pull an oracle card before leaving. You can also gift each person a crystal or a symbol of the work done in this circle.

Use your imagination and creativity to add your own personality to this ceremony. Trust your ideas, as they come from a higher source.

Play uplifting energizing music as people gather their things and prepare to leave.

CHAPTER 12
MAY MOON: HONOR MOTHER WITH FORGIVENESS

Full Moon Ceremony Honoring the Mother

Intention: In this ceremony we will celebrate and honor the healing essence of the Loving Mother by forgiving the women in our lives, including ourselves.

Women are the portal bringing life to the planet. Humans begin life in a woman, beamed through her womb. Women have the influence to create a loving community. The power that women possess is even greater than that. Women are guiding the human race to transcend to the next spiritual level.

Most of us aren't aware of our innate powers. We hide them beneath blocks and invisible walls we build around ourselves. Our true power lies within our love. However, the powerful love we possess is sometimes hidden by grudges and long- held resentments against ourselves, our mothers, and our sisters. We learned to hold these grudges at a younger age, and over time it became a regular practice. The only way to free the loving power within is by learning to let these grudges and resentments go.

When I was a little girl, I viewed my mother as an all-knowing being. She knew how to fix everything: scraped knees, torn dresses, broken hearts. When there was thunder and lightning and my sisters and I were afraid, Mom would light candles and we would huddle together on the couch and tell funny stories until the storm passed. She filled our souls with love and protection.

In my teen years I started to see my mother's flaws very clearly. I grew to resent her for being weak and marrying my abusive father. For years, I blamed her for my own problems.

One day, when I was well into my forties, I was asked a question that changed how I saw my mother forever: "How were your mother's dreams supported by the men in her life?" The answer hit me hard; she was never supported by anyone. I sobbed, hurting for her trapped all those years. I regretted my complaints about her, because I realized she never got to live her dreams.

I began to feel compassion for my mother. I forgave her for the choices she made that affected me. Then I forgave myself for being too hard on her. Relief came with forgiveness. I was no longer tethered to bad feelings from my past. I was freed to enjoy my life more deeply.

We all do the best we can with what we have. Our mothers and grand-mothers had situations we can't begin to understand. They didn't have the freedoms we have to express themselves, to connect with women, to expand their inner power.

Motherly love is a superpower. You don't have to give birth to possess the spirit of a loving mother. Your capacity for deep, big, expanding love gives you power. It tames men, heals children, and builds tight communities.

To deeply access that love, you have to release old resentments, anger, and grudges toward yourself and others. Holding onto that old stuff weighs you down. With forgiveness you can start fresh and allow your-self to flourish.

There are two very important things to know about forgiveness. First, forgiving someone doesn't imply that what they did was okay or has been forgotten. It's simply a way for you to remove the burden of anger and hurt from yourself to release it into the ether. When you forgive, it doesn't mean the person you forgave has a place in your life. You may forgive and at the same time choose not to have the person in your life if they're not good for you.

Second, forgiving someone doesn't have to be inspired by feelings. If you don't want to forgive emotionally, but intellectually you know that forgiving will heal your heart, simply make the choice to forgive and follow through with the action of forgiveness, and it will be done. Emotion will follow the decision and action.

In this moon ceremony we bring compassion and forgiveness to our mothers, grandmothers, sisters, and ourselves.

Set Your Sacred Space

Prepare your sacred space as directed in the chapter, "How to Use This Book."

Prepare your altar and add symbolic items such as a bouquet of roses, heart-shaped crystals or stones, and photos of some of the most famous mother figures such as Mother Teresa, the Blessed Mother or your own mother, grandmother, aunt, or sister.

You may choose to invite each member of your tribe to bring a photo of their most revered mother figure to add to the altar space. Call in your guides and higher self to bring positive energy to the space.

Ask your guides, "Please provide the wisdom to create a safe space and a loving experience for the women who attend. Help me give them exactly what they need at this time. Allow me to be the light and raise their vibrations."

Welcome

Welcome your tribe to the space, one by one. Thank each person for being here. Make them feel loved and welcome with a warm greeting and a hug. Clear each woman's energy as she enters. Invite her to find her space and get comfortable.

Opening

Open with a sound, chime, gong, or any audible indication that it's time to begin.

Ask everyone to become fully present. Help them settle in by asking them to inhale one deep breath, hold it, then slowly release it completely.

Give a loving smile and tell your tribe tonight's intention, then begin the ceremony. Remind everyone that this is a safe space, and anything shared in the circle is to be kept confidential.

You may want to tell a story of forgiveness from your past, or from a movie, or from someone you know. Or simply read the opening to this chapter as an introduction to the circle.

Your journal exercise will focus on the following:

1. **Name** one female figure in your life about whom you have a complaint.
2. **Identify** the positive aspects of forgiving this person.
3. **Tap into** your connection to a higher, loving power through meditation.

Journal Exercise

Make sure everyone has two small pieces of paper and a pen. Guide them through this exercise, allowing five minutes for each step.

Journaling Exercise #1: Name a female figure in your life you feel has wronged you in some way. Write down three things you choose to forgive them for. (This paper will be burned or destroyed at the end of the ceremony.)

Journaling Exercise #2: Forgive Write down the positive things that will come from forgiving this person. What will become easier for you when you forgive this person? How will it make your life better? (This paper will be reserved and kept as a reminder.)

Meditation

Note to reader: Take long pauses in between each visualization segment. Moments of silence will allow your tribe to better ease into the meditation.

This meditation will open our heart's passageway to love and forgiveness.

Close your eyes, settle in and get comfortable.

Take a deep breath in and release it slowly.

Lift your shoulders to the sky and release. Feel the burden of the day roll off of your shoulders.

Relax the muscles in your face.

Breath in and as you release, feel your face relax more.

Relax the muscles in your forehead.

Relax the muscles around your eyes.

Relax your jaw. Soften your lips.

Breathe in peace. Breathe out tension.

Place a hand on your heart space, on the center of your chest.

Breathe deeply in and feel your heart space rise into your hand.

Blow out through your mouth, pulling your belly button to your spine.

Now, visualize your heart space glowing a beautiful bright green light.

See this light expand larger and larger as it glows outside of your body and fills up the room.

Notice the capacity your heart has to shine light onto the other people in this space.

Now see your heart space light glowing and expanding outside of this space and filling up the sky and all of space.

Feel your grand capacity to shine your light to All That Is. Breath that feeling in.

Reader: Pause for a moment.

Now, visualize, in the sky above us, is a bright white ball of light shining down onto this circle, and shining into the crown of your head.

See the light fill you up from your head down to your heart and to the bottom of your toes.

Receive and accept this light. It is pure love.

Reader: Pause for a moment.

Feel as this pure white light fills you up and joins forces with your own green light.

Breath in the pure, loving feeling.

Feel your heart throb with pure love and peace.

Notice how that feels.

Now, put a tiny smile on your face.

Allow yourself to deeply feel love and peace.

Let's seal this in with one final deep breath in.

Release.

When you are ready, open your eyes.

We are complete.

Forgiveness Mantra

Now lead the circle to recite the following mantra with you three times.

Instruct them to first think of the person they chose to forgive, so the mantra is directed to that person. Suggest they feel the mantra in their heart with great love as they say it. Recite each line of the mantra first, and ask them to repeat after you:

- I'm sorry.
- Please forgive me as I forgive you.
- Let's forgive each other.
- I love you.

- Thank you.

Repeat the mantra three times. Then sit quietly for a moment.

Burn/Destroy Your Release Paper

Guide your tribe to destroy the journal exercise #1 paper, including the grudges they wish to release. This can be done either by safely burning the paper or by tearing it up and throwing it in a trash can.

Before destroying it tell yourself, "I now forgive the transgressions I no longer wish to hold onto."

Closing the Sacred Circle

Close the circle by guiding everyone to hold hands and lead a simple prayer of gratitude:

"We are grateful for the lessons learned from our mothers, grandmothers, sisters, and friends. We appreciate the love and open minds of the women here now. We are grateful for the practice of forgiveness, which brings us healing. We commit to bringing this loving energy into the world when we leave this ceremony. Let's close our eyes and smile as you think of one more thing you're grateful for right now."

You may pass the talking stick around, asking if anyone wants to share what came to them. When complete, thank everyone for coming. Tell them to take their time as they gather their things.

Remember to close your sacred space at the very end. You may do this by simply saying, "Sacred space now closed," or by reciting the Four Winds invocation offered in an earlier section in this book.

Be sure to clear yourself of any unwanted energies by smudging yourself from head to toe. This ceremony is a heavy one and you want to protect your energies from others.

Extra Special

You may add a special group prayer for someone in need, or for someone who is ill or suffering. Or you may say a group prayer for the world.

You can add to the experience by handing each person a rose or heart-shaped stone or crystal before they leave, saying, "You are important to the peace in this world."

Or invite them to pull an oracle card before leaving. Or gift each person a crystal or any other symbol of the work done in this circle. Use your imagination and creativity to add your own personality to this ceremony. Trust your ideas, as they come from a higher source.

Play uplifting energizing music as people gather their things and prepare to leave.

CHAPTER 13
JUNE MOON: BALANCE GIVING AND RECEIVING ABUNDANCE

Full Moon Ceremony – Balance Energy of Giving and Receiving Abundance

Intention: To balance the energy of giving and receiving abundance.

Everything is energy. Human essence is all energy, stuffed into a human body. Thoughts are energy and feelings are energy. This is clear when someone very happy enters a room, bringing good-feeling energy with them. It's also clear when someone in a bad mood enters your space and suddenly you feel bad.

All energy must flow or it gets stuck. The energies of abundance, such as love, money, and laughter are meant to flow in balance. The energy of giving and receiving abundance must freely flow in and freely out for us to be in harmony.

Some of us give too much or too little love. Love is an energy flow, and for one to have harmony love must flow both ways—in and out. Some of us give more than we're willing to receive. Others take more than they give. Either way, imbalance creates disharmony.

Sometimes we don't realize that we're withholding love from ourselves and others. There are times I catch myself wanting to give to someone and then a little monkey voice in the back of my head says, "That would be overly generous; don't do it." And then there are times someone wants to give to me, and I push it back, feeling guilty for taking.

It's beautiful to give without the expectation of anything in return. However, some people give to the point of being toxic and harmful to themselves and their families. This creates an imbalance and a feeling of being taken advantage of.

It's wonderful to be able to receive what people give you with great reverence. However, some people take more than they give, which also creates an imbalance and leads to feeling entitled or feeling shame. It also leads to a lack of opportunity, as the energy of abundance flowing in gets stuck.

The ideal balance is to give when you feel like giving and to receive happily when others give to you. Material gifts are symbols of love. Acts of kindness are symbols of love. Compliments are symbols of love. Love is a form of abundance.

In this ceremony we celebrate the balance of our capacity both for giving and receiving. We celebrate our mothers, our grandmothers, our sisters, and ourselves. We recognize the strength in our softness. We embrace the beauty of our love, and we cultivate a stronger bond of sisterhood among each other.

Set Your Sacred Space

Set up your sacred space as directed in the chapter, How to Use This Book.

Prepare your altar and add symbols of each of the four elements: earth, water, fire and air. Examples are a leaf, a rock or stick (earth); a small bowl of water from a local stream, lake, or ocean (water); a burning candle (fire); and burning incense (air).

You may add symbols of abundance, such as a $100 bill, a gold coin, anything heart-shaped, anything gold, a photo of a couple in love, etc. You may choose to invite your tribe to each bring a symbol of one of the four elements and/or a symbol of abundance to add to the altar space.

Call in your guides and higher self to bring positive energy into this space. Ask your guides, "Please provide me with the wisdom to create a safe space and a transformational experience for the women who attend. Help me give them exactly what they need at this time. Allow me to be the light and raise their vibrations."

Welcome

Welcome your tribe into the space, one by one. Thank each person for being here. Make her feel warm and welcome with a smile, a hug, and a compliment. Clear each woman's energy as she enters. Invite her to find her space and get comfortable.

Opening

Open with a sound, chime, gong, or any audible indication that it's time to begin.

Ask everyone to become fully present. Help them settle in by asking them to take one deep breath in, hold it, and slowly release it completely.

Give a loving smile and tell your tribe what tonight's intention is, and then begin the ceremony. Remind everyone that this is a safe space and anything shared in this circle is to be kept confidential.

Our journal exercise will focus on the following:

1. **Choose** where we want to GIVE more love and where we want to RECEIVE more love.
2. **Release** the block that keeps us from giving and receiving freely.

Journal Exercise

Make sure everyone has two small pieces of paper and a pen. Guide them through this exercise, allowing five minutes for each step.

Journaling Exercise #1: Choose Write down one area where you want to give more. This can include a relationship, your community, or yourself.

Next, write down one area in your life where you want to learn to allow yourself to receive more. This may be allowing others to help you, allowing money to flow to you, or allowing the world to give to you in some way. (This paper will be reserved and kept as a reminder.)

Journaling Exercise #2: Release Write down three things that may have been holding you back from giving or receiving. Then write down this question: Am I willing to release the things that hold me back? Then answer the question. (This paper will be burned or destroyed at the end of the ceremony.)

Meditation

Note to reader: Take long pauses in between segments. Moments of silence allow your tribe to better ease into the meditation.

Get into a comfortable position, either sitting up or laying down.

Take a deep breath in. Blow it out completely.

Take another deep breath in. And this time, release it completely by pulling your navel to your spine as you blow out.

And one more time; take a deep breath in.

Blow it out completely by sucking your stomach in as far as it can go.

Now, breathe normally. Notice your breath.

Is it becoming calmer?

Continue to focus on your breath.

Notice how it calms you as you place your attention on it.

Reader: Take a minute of silence here.

Settle into your body. Place a hand on your belly.

Notice your hand rise and fall with each breath.

Relax the muscles in your face.

Relax the muscles in your eyes.

Release any tension or tightness you might be holding in your jaw.

Allow any tension from the day to release and fall away from you.

Breathe in. Breathe out.

Notice how your body feels just being quiet.

Notice how it breathes entirely on it's own.

Notice how peaceful it is.

Reader: Take a minute of silence here.

Now imagine, in your mind's eye, that there is a beautiful golden light above your head. See this light shower into the top of your head, your crown chakra.

Notice the top of your head tingle as this light flows into it.

Now see the light shower down into your head. Watch it fill up your eyes, your ears, your throat.

Watch the light travel down into your heart space.

Then your stomach above your belly button.

Now see the golden light fill up your hips.

See the light travel down your legs, now filling your body from head to toe with a golden glow.

Now watch as the light travels out of the bottoms of your feet and deep into the center of the earth, grounding you to mother nature.

Watch the golden light fill up the cavern in the center of the earth and then bounce right back up through the ground and back into the soles of your feet.

You are now a glowing ember of beautiful golden light.

Enjoy the feeling of being grounded.

Breathe in. Breathe out.

Notice how you are always given a breath, just when you need it. Easily, naturally.

Notice how generous the breaths are. They never hold back.

Notice how your body is always there for you.

Know that everything you need is always given to you, all you have to do is allow yourself to receive it.

Just as you allow yourself to receive the breaths, you can allow receiving of everything in life.

Breathe in the feeling of knowing that you are always provided for.

Breathe out any feeling of lack.

Now place your focus on your heart space. Notice how your heart glows with the golden light, as if it's a giant sunshine right in your heart.

Allow your heart's light to activate your enthusiasm to generously give to others.

Feel the energy of the light in your heart grow.

In your mind's eye, see the glow of your heart space expand outside of your body, and watch as it continues to expand to fill up the entire room.

Now see your heart's light expand beyond the town you are in.

Now see your heart's light expand beyond the country you are in.

Now see your heart's light expand beyond the entire earth.

Feel that connection to all-that-is, as your loving energy is generously expanded.

Reader: Take a minute of silence here.

Now, in your mind's eye, notice that there is a light energy source beaming down from heaven as it showers on you, lovingly combining with your own golden light source.

Bathe in the light as you breathe the collaborative light in and out.

Relax.

Enjoy the feeling of giving. Enjoy the feeling of receiving.

Know that you deserve all the love you are given.

And you deserve to give all the love that you contain.

Breathe in the feeling of being at one with all.

Breathe out.

We are complete.

Take your time getting up.

Wiggle your fingers and toes.

Move slowly.

Take this energy with you into the next segment of your day.

Burn/Destroy Your Release Paper

Guide your tribe to destroy the journal exercise #2 paper, including those items they wish to release. This can be done either by safely burning the paper, or by tearing it up and throwing it in a trash can. Before destroying it tell yourself, "I now release these things I no longer wish to hold onto."

Closing the Sacred Circle

Close the circle by guiding everyone to hold hands and lead a simple prayer of gratitude:

"We are grateful for this time of healing. We are appreciative for the love and open minds of the women here right now. We commit to bringing this beautiful energy into the world when we leave this ceremony today. Now let's all close our eyes and smile as you think of one more thing you're grateful for right now."

Thank everyone for coming. Tell them to take their time as they gather their things.

Remember to close your sacred space at the very end. You may do this by simply saying, "Sacred space now closed," or by reciting the Four Winds invocation offered in an earlier section of this book.

Cleanse your own energy by smudging yourself from head to toe, releasing any unwanted energies you may have picked up from your tribe during the ceremony.

Extra Special

You may add to the experience by inviting them to pull an oracle card before leaving.

You may add a special group prayer for someone in need, or for someone who is ill or suffering. Or you may say a group prayer for the world.

Gift each person something that may be symbolic of the work done in this ceremony. Play uplifting energizing music as people gather their things and prepare to leave.

Use your imagination and creativity to add your own personality to this ceremony. Trust your ideas, as they come from a higher source.

CHAPTER 14
JULY MOON: BALANCE THE MASCULINE AND FEMININE

Full Moon Ceremony - Balancing the Masculine and Feminine Energies

Intention: To balance our masculine and feminine energies.

Note: If you have been wanting to bring men into your sacred space, this is the perfect ceremony to do it.

Every one of us contains both masculine and feminine energy. When both energies are in balance, we have healthy bodies and minds. We are in harmony, and that harmony extends into our communities and our world.

Masculine energies embody logic, reason, strength, action, strategy. Feminine energies embody intuition, nurturing, healing, creation, spontaneity.

When men have their energies perfectly balanced, they contain within them the feminine energy of nurturing. You see this when they become fathers or get a puppy.

When women have their energies perfectly balanced, they contain within them the masculine energy of strategy. You see this when they become business owners or create something.

When these energies are out of balance we have inner conflict, power struggles, war, and emotional crisis. It begins within us in our lives and spills out into the collective world. When these energies are in balance, we are in harmony.

When your feminine energy is wounded, it manifests in the form of desperation, neediness, drama, depletion of energy, or depression. But when your divine feminine is in balance, you are powerful, loving, and magnetic, attracting what you want to yourself.

When your masculine energy is wounded, there is conflict, fear, and war. But when your divine masculine energy is in balance, you take decisive action to protect and provide for your family and the community.

The world becomes out of balance when we as the collective are out of balance.

Our world is a little out of balance right now, and we are changing it by doing this work.

Thousands of years ago the pendulum swung far too into masculine energy. It's been out of balance this way for centuries. But it is starting to change, and the pendulum is beginning to swing in the other direction. The practice we do in this ceremony will gently balance and activate the energies within us into a healthy state.

Set Your Sacred Space

Set up your sacred space as directed in the chapter, How to Use This Book.

Prepare your altar and add symbolic items that embody both feminine and masculine energies. Examples are flowers, sticks, stones and bones, heart-shaped items, something soft and something hard.

Clear your sacred space of any unwanted energy. Call in your guides and higher self to bring positive energy to the space.

Ask your guides, "Please provide the wisdom to create a powerful experience for the people who join me in this practice. Help me guide them in a way that will generate balance within them. Allow me to be the light and raise their vibrations."

Welcome

Welcome your tribe into the space, one by one. Thank each person for being here. Make them feel warmly loved by giving a hug and a compliment. Clear each person's energy with sage or Palo Santo as they enter. Invite them to find a space and get comfortable.

Opening

Open with a sound, chime, gong, or any audible indication that it's time to begin.

Ask everyone to become fully present. Help them settle in by asking them to take one deep breath in, hold it, and slowly release it completely.

Give a loving smile and tell your tribe what tonight's intention is, then begin the ceremony. Feel free to read the introduction at the top of this page and add any additional thoughts or research you may have. Remind everyone that this is a safe space and anything shared in this circle is to be kept confidential.

In this ceremony we will activate balance of the divine feminine and masculine within each person, focusing on the following exercises:

1. **Choose** what you want to embody.
2. **Decide** what you want to release.
3. **Meditate** to activate/balance masculine and feminine energies.

Journal Exercise

Make sure everyone has two small pieces of paper and a pen. Guide them through this exercise, allowing five minutes for each step.

Journaling Exercise #1: Create Choose one masculine or feminine trait you wish to embody more of within yourself and write it in the format beginning "I am."

- I am forgiving.

- I am loving.
- I am strong.
- I am disciplined.
- I am in tune with my intuition.
- I am a healer.
- I am focused.

(This paper will be reserved, kept in your wallet, or taped on a wall as a reminder.)

Journaling exercise #2:   Release We all have negative thoughts that plague our minds. Often, it's a worry, a grudge, or a regret. Write down one negative recurring concern you're willing to release.

(This paper will be burned or destroyed at the end of the ceremony.)

Meditation

Get yourself comfortable, either sitting up or laying down.

Close your eyes.

Allow your body to sink down into the earth and feel yourself getting into a deep relaxation.

Place a hand on your belly.

Take a deep breath in, feeling your belly rise. Hold for a count of three.

One.

Two.

Three.

When you exhale, pull your navel to your spine and push out all the stale air that you have been holding.

Take another deep breath, hold it…., then release it completely by activating your abdominal muscles, pulling your navel to your spine as you blow out.

Now place your focus on the soles of your feet.

Imagine that you have thick, healthy roots growing out of the bottom of your feet. Visualize these roots burrowing through the ground and watch as they travel all the way to the center of the earth.

In the center of the earth there is a huge, beautiful crystal cavern.

In the center of the cavern ceiling hangs a glistening clear quartz crystal.

This crystal was formed from healing waters and contains ancient codes of wisdom.

Visualize wrapping your roots around the crystal three times.

One.

Two.

Three.

Now, feel the energy of the crystal flow like a river, traveling up through your roots, to the bottoms of your feet, flowing up your spine and out of the top of your head.

Feel the river of energy activate circulation through your spine.

Reader: pause for a minute to allow this to resonate.

Place your focus on the top of your head, your crown chakra. Notice the skin on your head tingle as the blood circulates.

Now, in your mind's eye, see above your head, in the sky, a large glowing fireball, our beautiful sun.

Allow the powerful fire of the sun to penetrate the crown of your head.

Visualize this bright light and warmth travel down from your head to the center of your eyes. Notice how it fills you with light and warmth.

Now see the glowing fire travel down to your throat.

Now watch as it travels to your heart center.

Now see it shower down to your solar plexus above your navel.

Now see the glowing light fill up your abdomen.

Feel the warmth and light travel to the bottom of your spine and down your legs, to your ankles and watch as the fiery light shoots out of the bottoms of your feet.

Notice your body tingle with the energy of this activating fire from head to toe.

Reader: pause for a moment.

Now, imagine that the energy from the beautiful crystal is flowing upward from the earth, into the bottom of your feet and up your spine.

Visualize the sun's fiery energy wrapping around the crystal's water energy, forming a double helix.

Reader: Pause for a minute to allow for this to formulate in their minds.

Visualize these two energies twirling around each other and dancing together, up and down your spine.

Feel the two energies shooting up and down your spine, wrapped around each other in unity.

Breath through it.

Reader: Pause for a minute.

Now take a deep breath in. Blow it out completely.

Notice the activation and balancing of your divine energies.

Notice the feeling of balance, strength, nurturing and harmony.

Let's take one last deep breath in and gently blow it out.

We are complete.

Slowly open your eyes.

Wiggle your fingers and toes.

Take your time moving out from meditation.

Burn/Destroy Your Release Paper

Guide your tribe to destroy the journal exercise #2 paper, including the items they wish to release. This can be done by safely burning the paper, or by tearing it up and throwing it in a trash can. Before destroying it tell yourself, "I now release this concern I no longer wish to hold onto."

Closing the Sacred Circle

Close the circle by guiding everyone to hold hands and leading a simple prayer of gratitude:

"We are grateful for this time together. We appreciate the love and open minds of the people here right now. We commit to bringing balance of the feminine and masculine into the world when we leave this ceremony today. Close your eyes and smile as you think of one thing you're grateful for right now."

You may pass the talking stick around, asking if anyone wants to share what came to them. When complete, thank everyone for coming. Tell them to take their time as they gather their things.

Remember to close your sacred space at the very end. You may do this by simply saying, "Sacred space now closed," or by reciting the Four Winds invocation offered in an earlier section of this book.

Extra Special

You can add to the experience by including a sound healing after the meditation (either live or recorded).

You may add a short yoga exercise, or Tai Chi, or stretching exercise before the meditation. You may say a group prayer or invocation for someone in need, or for the collective as a whole.

Invite them to do a card pulling before leaving, or gift each person a crystal or another symbol of the work done in this circle. Play uplifting energizing music as people gather their things and prepare to leave. You might encourage everyone to get up and dance together.

For this ceremony, you may want to provide a rose or flower to each male and a stone or leaf to each woman before they leave.

CHAPTER 15

AUGUST MOON: WHO YOU REALLY ARE

Full Moon Ceremony

Intention: The intention of this ceremony is to connect you to the essence of who you really are.

The essence of who you really are contains your grandest potential—a potential so large you may not be aware of it or trust in it.

Your grand potential is what you came to earth to do. For some, it's to be a loving leader of your community, or a mother leading a family. For others, it's to save the world with the next big invention. And yet for others it's to impact people through creative works. The size or scale of your potential doesn't matter; bringing it to life is important.

Most of us haven't come close to reaching our grandest potential. One reason is that it often takes time. It requires a long journey and a collection of knowledge and wisdom. The greater the potential the longer it takes, and as humans we are very impatient.

Many of us are held back from our grand potential because we don't allow ourselves to be who we really are. Other people's ideas of us take over. We lack trust in the importance of our own desires and worthiness.

Every one of us, at one time or another, has been prevented from reaching our grand potential because we were held back by lack of trust. Our grand potential is hidden by our lack of trust in our instincts, the validity of our own dreams and desires, or the things that light our fires.

Ultimately, we lack trust in our worthiness. Fear whispers in our ears, "What if they don't like me anymore? What if they disapprove, or what if I'm not worthy?"

Here's what you need to know: your fear of not being good enough is not real, because you're perfect just the way you are. You must learn to trust your ideas, dreams, and desires.

I'd like to give you a fresh point of view, another way of looking at yourself. A truth that you may not have thought of.

Think back to the day you were born, when you were delivered from your mother's womb and brought into this world. On that day you were perfect, just like the trees, the moon, and the ocean. You were a perfect seed of potential, like a sunflower. A sunflower begins life as a seed that contains within it great potential to be beautiful as it grows up.

You were born perfect and that has not changed! You contain the same essence and potential today as you did on the day you came into this world, a seedling of what was possible.

Today's meditation will help you feel ready to step into your grand potential, recognizing your worthiness to do so.

Set Your Sacred Space

Set up your sacred space as directed in the chapter, How to Use This Book.

Set up your altar and add symbolic items such as seedlings, pink or red crystals, a photo of a baby or of someone great and inspirational, and other reminders of birth and grandness. You may invite your tribe to bring a photo of themselves as a baby or small child to add to the altar to remind them of their innate grandness.

Clear your sacred space of any unwanted energy. Call in your guides and higher self to bring positive loving energy to the space. Ask your guides, "Please provide me with the wisdom to create a powerful experience for those who come. Help me guide them to understand their grandness and worthiness. Allow me to be the light and raise their vibrations."

Welcome

Welcome your tribe into the space, one by one. Thank each person for coming. Make them feel greatly loved with a personal greeting and compliment, such as, "I'm so glad you are here. You look beautiful tonight." Clear each person's energy as they enter. Invite them to find their space and get comfortable.

Opening

Open with a sound, chime, gong, or any audible indication that it's time to begin.

Ask everyone to become fully present. Help them settle in by asking them to take a deep breath in, hold it, and slowly release it completely.

Give a loving smile and tell your tribe what tonight's intention is, then begin the ceremony. Remind everyone that this is a safe space and anything shared in this circle is to be kept confidential.

You may read the introduction to this ceremony and add your own personal story. A personal story adds to the impact of your ceremony. For example, you could tell a story of how you were prevented from doing something you dreamed of, and one day you broke through that resistance and made your dream happen.

In this ceremony we will guide you on a visualization that will connect you to the essence of who you really are. We will do the following:

1. **Explore** the things you dream of doing.
2. **Discover** and **release** one thing that holds you back.
3. **Meditate** with a visualization that will guide you to your true essence.

Journal Exercise

Make sure everyone has two small pieces of paper and a pen. Guide them through this exercise, allowing five minutes for each step.

Journaling Exercise #1: Explore Think back to what you dreamed of as a child. Write down five or more things you dreamed then. These can be material things, a place you dreamed of going to, someone you wanted to become, something you wanted to create, or anything you desired. (This paper will be reserved and kept as a reminder.)

Allow five minutes of silence, as this takes some deep digging. After three minutes of silence, encourage your tribe by saying, "Dig deeper now. What else did you dream of?"

After five more minutes, ask your tribe to look at their list and circle the dreams they still have as an adult. (This paper will be kept as a reminder.)

Journaling exercise #2: Discover/Release Write **Discover** and **Release** on a piece of paper. Look at the dreams you circled on your first piece of paper and write down one thing that held you back from bringing them to life. (This paper will be burned or destroyed at the end of the ceremony.)

Meditation

Note: Read slowly with long pauses in between each sentence. This allows your tribe to take the time to integrate the visualization.

Get in a comfortable position. Close your eyes and take a deep breath in. Place your hand on your belly; feel it rise and fall with your breath.

Take another deep breath in and hold it for a count of three, two, one. Release the breath completely by pulling your belly button to your spine.

Relax the muscles in your forehead. Relax the muscles in your eyes. Relax your jaw. Feel the tension gently release from your body.

Now, place your attention on the soles of your feet. Imagine there are strong, healthy roots growing from the soles of your feet. Watch as they burrow into the earth below you.

See your roots as they travel deep into the center of the earth, and in the center there's a large network of tree roots from every tree on earth!

In the center of the network there is one large tree trunk connecting all earthly tree roots. Visualize as you wrap your roots around this mother tree trunk three times.

One.

Two.

Three.

Breathe in and feel the energy of all earth's trees flow into your roots and up to the soles of your feet.

Note to reader: Pause here for a minute.

Feel the earthly energy of the trees flow up your spine and travel to the top of your head. Take a breath in and a breath out.

Remember a moment when you felt truly connected to *all that is.* Think of a time you were overcome with joy and your vibration was high.

Remember a time when you were high on life, in love with someone or something, living in the moment.

Note to reader: Pause here for a minute.

As you recall this wonderful time, squeeze your middle finger and thumb together, and hold tightly as you feel that memory in your heart.

Now release the hold and take a breath in and out.

Let's do that again. Think of that happy, high-on-life memory. Feel the joy of it in your body. As you feel the joy, squeeze your middle finger and thumb together.

In your mind's eye, see yourself in that happy time, feeling powerful in the flow of life.

Feel the joy inside you as you press your finger and thumb together. Place that feeling of love, joy, and flow into your finger and thumb.

Now release.

You can revisit this feeling anytime by pressing your middle finger and thumb together, whenever you need to be reminded of your ability to feel great joy and flow.

Note to reader: Pause here for a minute.

Now imagine that you're walking barefoot in a forest that meets the sea.

Feel your bare feet walking on the soft grass beneath a large canopy of trees.

Notice your connection to the earth as you walk on the grass toward the ocean and sand in the distance.

Step on the warm sand as you get closer to the water. Feel the sun on your shoulders.

Notice the ocean waves gently lapping on the shore. The water is a calm glassy deep blue inviting you to step in. You walk in the water up to your knees. The saltwater feels warm on your skin.

You notice your reflection dancing on the surface of the water.

The mirrored image is you, but a larger grander version of you. The image transforms into a moving picture of you, a grander version of yourself.

What is the grander version of you doing in the moving reflection? Are you dancing, laughing, teaching, painting, writing, sky diving?

Notice what you're doing in your grander version and enjoy it.

Note to reader: Pause here for a minute.

See the reflection of your face and notice it glowing. A halo of light emanates from your head and body. The essence of you is free to express who you really are. Feel the pure love of this moment.

Press your middle finger and your thumb together and feel into the powerful essence of who you really are.

Know that anytime you want to remember who you really are you can press your middle finger and thumb together and revisit the feeling.

Bring your attention back to the here and now, in this time and space. Take a deep breath in. Release.

With your next breath, breath in the essence of you as it fills your entire body, like a glowing light.

Allow that light to expand to every corner of your body. Feel the light fill your ears, arms, hands, stomach, ribs, legs, and toes.

Your entire body is now filled with light. Allow the light to expand beyond your body and fill the space outside yourself into the world around you.

Notice how good it feels to be free to be you.

Note to reader: Pause here for a minute.

Let's seal this feeling in with a final deep breath in.

Blow it out with an audible sigh, *ahh.* We are complete.

Burn/Destroy Your Release Paper

Guide your tribe to destroy the journal exercise #2 paper, including what they wish to release. This can be done either by safely burning the paper or by tearing it up and throwing it in a trash can. This can be done together as a group or in private. Before destroying it tell yourself, "I now release those things I no longer wish to hold onto."

Closing the Sacred Circle

Ask if anyone wants to share their experience tonight. Encourage them to share what their dreams were and what held them back. Ask if the writing exercise or meditation helped them discover something new about themselves. Feel free to share your own experience as well.

Close the circle by guiding everyone to hold hands and lead a simple prayer of gratitude:

"We are grateful for this time of healing. We appreciate the love and open minds of the women here right now. We commit to bringing our grand energy to the world when we leave the ceremony today. Let's all close our eyes and smile as you think of one thing you're grateful for right now."

Thank everyone for coming. Tell them to take their time as they gather their things.

Remember to close your sacred space at the very end. You may do this by simply saying, "Sacred space now closed," or by reciting the Four Winds invocation offered in an earlier section of this book.

Extra Special

You may add a special group prayer for someone in need, or for someone who is ill or suffering. Or you may say a group prayer for the world.

You can add to the experience by handing each person a rose or heart-shaped stone or crystal before they leave, saying, "It's amazing watching you step into your grand potential." You may also invite them to pull an oracle card before leaving.

Use your imagination and creativity to add your own personality to this ceremony. Trust your ideas, as they come from a higher source.

Play uplifting energizing music as people gather their things and prepare to leave. End with playful dance music and invite everyone to dance to a song or two.

CHAPTER 16
SEPTEMBER MOON: EXPAND ABUNDANCE

Full Moon Ceremony – Expand Your Capacity for Abundance

Intention: Expand your capacity to receive the abundance that is available to you.

As we move into a new season, new opportunities will open. This ceremony will help you open to receive abundance as it's offered to you. This may surprise you, but there are areas in your life where at times you say "no" to abundance without realizing it.

The word abundance describes all the wonderful things life has to offer you. Abundance is love, money, achievement, joy, laughter, food, comfort, nature, and everything else that makes living beautiful.

Everyone is very good at receiving abundance in one area while unconsciously blocking abundance in other areas. For example, you might be very good at attracting and receiving love in your life, but when it comes to money you never have enough. On the other hand, you may be great at calling money into your life, but you have blocks to receiving love.

Most blocks to abundance can be traced back to childhood. If you were raised in a home where your parents felt there was never enough money, you may have developed a blockage to receiving money. If your family wasn't loving and accepting, you may have developed a blockage to love. These blockages are often hidden. You have to be aware of the possibility of blockage to notice you're saying no to love, money, and other things you'd love to have.

When someone compliments you, do you say. "Thank you," or do you say, "Oh no, this old thing?" Being unable to graciously receive a compliment is a form of a blockage to receiving love. Being unwilling to graciously accept money or gifts from others is a form of blockage to both money and love.

In the spring of 2020, some of my professional musician friends had a jam session in the parking lot of my art gallery. We had been closed due to the Covid lockdowns and I was excited to do something fun. We had a small outdoor concert and invited a small group of friends to enjoy the music. To my surprise, many people bought artwork from my gallery that night. At the end of the night, I decided to share the wealth with the musicians who had played for free. They hadn't been able to make money playing music due to the Covid shutdown, and I was happy to be able to give them something.

I called the first musician to my office and held out a wad of cash for him. He pushed it away, saying, "No, no, I can't take that. I was just having fun!" I insisted, and he reluctantly took the money.

I called the second musician to my office and handed her cash. She also pushed it away saying, "Oh no, I can't accept that." I insisted, and she finally took the money.

Then I called in the third musician and held my hand out to him with cash, also expecting him to push it away. Instead, he accepted the money, held it to his heart, and graciously said, "Thank you."

The next day I pondered this and wondered whether I accepted abundance when life tried to hand it to me, or if I pushed it away. I realized that if you turn down abundance in small ways, you probably also turn it down in big ways. If you can't receive graciously and say, "Thank you," the Universe will stop offering it to you.

Everything we do is habit, and every habit generates a result. The great news is you can shift the unconscious habit of saying no to what you really want. You just need to notice you're doing it. When you catch yourself the moment you're blocking abundance, you can shift the block by saying, "Thank you," and accepting it into your life.

You can also shift into a new habit of receiving by taking your mind and heart to a past time when you received abundance. Think back to a time you held an adorable baby or puppy, or when you had a joyful moment with a loved one, or when you received a gift of something you wanted for a long time. Now take the energy of happily receiving and project it into future desires.

From this point forward, when anything is offered to you, say, "Thank you!" and then invite future opportunities by saying, "More, please!"

Set Your Sacred Space

Set up your sacred space as directed in the chapter, How to Use This Book.

Set up your altar and add symbolic items for abundance, such as a $100 bill, a citrine crystal, a healthy plant, a photo of a couple in love, a piece of gold, a green or gold candle, and other reminders of great abundance. Then clear your sacred space of any unwanted energy.

Call in your guides and higher self to bring positive loving energy to the space. Ask your guides, "Please provide me with the wisdom to create a powerful experience for those who come. Help me guide them to understand their worthiness for great abundance. Allow me to be the light and raise their vibrations."

Welcome

Welcome your tribe into the space, one by one. Thank each person for being here. Tell each one as they arrive that they make your life more abundant. Give them a compliment and a hug. Clear each person's energy as they enter. Invite them to find a space and get comfortable.

Opening

Open with a sound, chime, gong, or any audible indication that it's time to begin.

Ask everyone to become fully present. Help them settle in by asking them to take a deep breath in, hold it, and completely release it slowly.

Give a loving smile and tell your tribe what tonight's intention is, then begin the ceremony. Remind everyone that this is a safe space, and anything shared in this circle is to be kept confidential. You are welcome to read the introduction in this chapter or add your own story of receiving or not receiving abundance.

This ceremony will expand your capacity to receive abundance in all areas of your life. We will:

1. **Identify** our blocks to abundance.
2. **Remember** past experiences where we successfully called abundance into our lives.
3. **Project** the vibration of past abundance into our future desires.

Journal Exercise

Make sure everyone has two small pieces of paper and a pen. Guide them through the exercise, allowing five minutes for each step.

Journaling Exercise #1: Identify Blocks We begin by writing a list of five things you desire in your life. It can be the improvement of a relationship, material items such as a car or home, resolution of a problem, new habits you wish to form, an achievement, or anything you desire.

Next to each desire, write a word or phrase that describes what has been blocking you from fully receiving it. You will destroy this piece of paper after the ceremony as a symbol of letting go of blocks that keep you from your desires.

Journaling exercise #2: Remember Write down three instances when you called abundance into your life. This could be when you met someone you love, had a child, got that dream job, had your first kiss, got a promotion, achieved something you worked for, or any good thing you received.

Next to each example of abundance, write a word or phrase that describes how you felt when you received it. You will keep this piece of paper as a reminder that you're capable of receiving abundance.

Meditation

This guided visualized meditation will expand your capacity to receive abundance.

We begin with relaxation and grounding. You'll be led to visualize using your imagination to achieve more powerful states of receiving.

Get into a comfortable position. You may lie down or sit up.

Close your eyes. Allow your body to sink into the earth, relaxing deeply. Place a hand on your belly.

Take a deep breath in, feeling your belly rise and hold it for a count of three.

When you exhale, pull your navel to your spine and push out any stale air you've been holding. Take another deep breath, hold it for a count of three, and release it completely.

Move your attention to the soles of your feet. Imagine that you have thick, healthy roots growing from the soles of your feet.

In your mind's eye, visualize your roots burrowing deep into the ground and watch as they travel all the way to the center of the earth. In the center of the earth there's a huge cavern containing a lush, green forest where all roots from the earth's trees connect.

In the center of the forest a giant Tree of Life connects to every tree in the world.

Visualize wrapping your roots around the Tree of Life three times.

One.

Two.

Three.

Now, feel yourself absorbing life force energy from the Tree of Life and feel the life force travel up through your roots into the soles of your feet, flowing up your spine and out the top of your head.

Notice how this energy activates a gentle vibration through your body.

Note to reader: *Pause here for a minute.*

Bring your attention back to your breath. Notice the abundance of breath you contain. You always have another breath coming easily and without effort.

Notice the rise and fall of your belly with each breath you take.

Now imagine that you're standing on the edge of a narrow river. The water is warm and crystal clear—so clear you can see the bottom of the river, which is lined with clear quartz crystals.

Notice a small golden rowboat waiting for you by the river's edge. Climb into the golden boat and point it downstream.

Glide down the river, noticing how easy it is to go with the flow of the river. No paddling is required.

Note to reader: *Pause here for a minute.*

As you float downstream, you see on the riverbank images of all the abundance you've received in your life: your first kiss, kindnesses you've received, people who are most important to you, your favorite food.

Take a moment to visualize all the big and small forms of abundance currently in your life.

Note to reader: *Pause here for a minute.*

Continue floating downstream and watch as you float past the faces of everyone you love: family, friends, mentors, community members.

What faces are you seeing? Notice how many people there are that you love.

Now see on the river's edge all the pets, children, and wild animals you've loved.

You continue to glide downstream and float past images of your most precious achievements and the things you're most proud of.

You see all the money that has flowed to you. You float past memories of adventures and vacations you've had.

Continue floating as you see images of moments of joy and laughter you've experienced.

Feel yourself going with the flow of the river's gentle current. Notice how easily you float downstream. You feel free and joyful.

Note to reader: Pause here for a minute.

Now place your attention in the distance ahead of your boat. See ahead where the narrow river opens into a large ocean.

In the ocean just beyond the river's opening, you see a small patch of land called the Island of Plenty.

The Island of Plenty contains all the abundance you dream of calling into your life: all the love, friendship, money, future achievements, laughter, and joy. All the material things you want are also there: the dream house, the car, vacations, and toys.

See all the wonderful things you want to call into your life—love, laughter, money, confidence, and the person you've wanted to grow into for so long.

All your dreams and desires are right there, and your boat is moving closer and closer to it.

Note to reader: Pause here for a minute.

You drift to the opening in the large ocean, but then your golden boat stops! It's stuck on something. See yourself looking into the clear water.

Notice that a small black rock is holding your boat back.

Climb out of the boat and step into the warm waist-deep water, which feels wonderful to stand in. See yourself reach into the water and pick up the black rock. Hold it in the palm of your hand. Feel your palm tingle as you hold it.

The other side of the black rock has a word etched on it. The word describes what is keeping you stuck.

Turn the rock over and read what's written there. The first word that pops into your head is what you see.

Note to reader: *Pause here for a minute.*

Put a tiny smile on your face. It's funny, isn't it? It's so simple, that thing that's been blocking you from your abundance.

Take the rock and throw it as far as you can into the sky and watch it disappear. Climb back into your golden boat and float toward the Land of Plenty.

Notice how easy it is now to glide toward everything you want.

Your boat drifts gently, and nothing stops you. Notice the great feeling of ease, the great feeling of allowing.

As you approach the island shore, look at all the abundance waiting for you—happy faces, great experiences: money, joy, achievements. Accept all the abundance!

Say *yes* to it. Feel appreciation for it in your heart as you say, "Thank you!"

Note to reader: *Pause here for a minute.*

Take one last deep breath in. Release it slowly.

Open your eyes; we are complete.

Burn/Destroy Your Blocks

Guide your tribe to destroy the journal exercise #1 paper, including those items they wish to release. This can be done either by safely burning the paper, or by tearing it up and throwing it in a trashcan. Before destroying it tell yourself, "I now release those blocks I no longer wish to keep."

Closing the Sacred Circle

You may pass the talking stick around and ask if anyone wants to share their blocks, or if they want to share the impact meditation had on them. Assure everyone that what is shared in the circle is sacred and will be kept confidential.

When someone shares, listen without comment. Thank them for being vulnerable and then ask the circle if anyone else wants to share.

Close the circle by guiding everyone to hold hands and lead a simple prayer of gratitude:

"We are grateful for this time of healing. We appreciate the love and open minds of those gathered here right now. We commit to bringing the energy of abundance into the world when we leave this ceremony today. Let's all close our eyes and smile as you think of one thing you're grateful for right now."

Thank everyone for coming. Tell them to take their time as they gather their things.

Remember to close your sacred space at the very end. You may do this by simply saying, "Sacred space now closed," or by reciting the Four Winds invocation offered in an earlier section of this book.

Extra Special

You may add a special group prayer for someone in need, or for someone who is ill or suffering. Or you may say a group prayer for the world.

You can add to the experience by handing each person a flower, heart-shaped stone, or crystal before they leave, saying "Your river of abundance is now flowing." You may also invite them to pull an oracle card before leaving.

End with playful dance music and invite everyone to dance to a song or two. Use your imagination and creativity to add your own personality to this ceremony. Trust your ideas, as they come from a higher source.

CHAPTER 17

OCTOBER MOON: KEEP YOUR FIRE ALIVE

Full Moon Ceremony – Keep Your Fire Alive

Intention: Prepare for the darker days of winter by activating your inner fire.

October brings us from the end of summer to the start of winter. This is the time to prepare and preserve for the darker days of winter. In ancient times, if you didn't properly prepare for colder days ahead, it meant certain death. You were wise to hunt and preserve food in advance and to keep the fires alive all winter.

For us here and now we prepare for the internal work of going within. We prepare to handle seasonal depression, holiday strife with family, and the somber feelings that come with going deep within as we spend more time in darkness.

Winter is the perfect time to do shadow work. Shadow work is looking deep inside yourself to identify parts of yourself that you're blind to. Shadow work reveals aspects of your personality you reject, often unknowingly. What you despise in others may unknowingly be within yourself.

For example, if as a child you were yelled at for speaking up, you might have developed a fear of speaking your truth. And now, when others around you speak their truth confidently, it may trigger anger or other undesirable action. You may have been doing this unconsciously your entire life until you go within and do the shadow work. Many people work with coaches or shamans to guide them through shadow work which can be emotional, especially for those who have suffered trauma and abuse.

An easy way to prepare for shadow work on your own is to notice when you're triggered by the actions of others. Being triggered shows itself in many ways. One way is when interaction with someone creates a strong, negative reaction in you. Just notice it and write it in a journal. When you're triggered, notice it without judgment.

When feeling triggered, ask yourself questions, such as the following:

- Does this reveal something I'm hiding in myself?
- What makes it difficult for me to be around a certain person?
- Do I have some of those undesirable traits myself?
- Am I less confident when I'm around a particular person? If so, why?

Noticing, asking questions, and writing them down helps reveal parts of your shadow self. Sometimes just recognizing it helps to dissolve it. Other times, recognition provides information we need to move toward resolution in the future.

Some of the greatest lessons come from recognizing shadow parts of ourselves we keep hidden away. When we bring shadows to the surface, we can heal them and with healing comes expansion and growth. With this work, relationships are more harmonious, and we experience greater peace and joy. It's worth the effort as it will make life better.

This month's moon ceremony will prepare you for the darker days of winter by activating your inner fire. After the meditation you will feel bright and powerful.

Set Your Sacred Space

Create your sacred space as directed in the chapter, How to Use This Book.

Set up your altar and add symbolic items for the season such as a pumpkins, brightly colored leaves, or a cornucopia. Add extra elements of fire by adding more candles to your altar.

Clear your sacred space of any unwanted energy. Call in your guides and higher self to bring positive energy to the space. Ask your guides, "Please provide me with the wisdom to create a loving and gentle experience for the women who attend. Help me give them exactly what they need right now. Allow me to guide them to grow their own light and raise their vibrations."

Welcome

Welcome your tribe into your space, one by one. Thank each person for being here. Make each one feel deeply loved with a warm, personal greeting. Clear each woman's energy as she enters. Invite her to find her space and get comfortable.

Opening

Open with a sound, chime, gong, or any audible indication that it's time to begin.

Ask everyone to become fully present. Help them settle in by asking them to take one deep breath in, hold it, and slowly release it completely.

You may choose to set the mood by guiding everyone to chant Om together. Ask them to take a deep breath and on the exhale, start the Om chant by making the long O sound, followed by the M sound. Encourage your tribe to repeat the chant three times together, allowing the sound to resonate and vibrate within them. After the third Om chant, sit in stillness for a moment to absorb the effects of the practice. Ask them to notice any shifts in their body, mind, and energy. (**Note:** you may find an Om chant on YouTube as a guide for chanting if that makes it easier for you. Or practice this alone before the ceremony.)

Give a loving smile and tell your tribe what tonight's intention is, then begin the ceremony. Remind everyone that this is a safe space and anything shared in the circle is to be kept confidential.

In this ceremony we will:

1. **Release** one trigger we wish to eliminate.
2. **Identify** one response we wish to substitute for the trigger.

Journal Exercise

Make sure everyone has two small pieces of paper and a pen. Guide them through this exercise, allowing five minutes for each exercise.

Journaling Exercise #1: Release Begin by writing one trigger you wish to release. "Name one thing that someone does that triggers me so much I have a strong, negative emotional response." (This paper will be burned or destroyed at the end of the ceremony.)

Journaling exercise #2: Identify Name one trigger you want to replace. Examples: patience, silence, kindness, confidence to speak up, or the opposite of what you wrote down on your "release" paper. (This paper will be kept in your wallet or placed somewhere in your home so you see it often.)

Meditation

The intention of today's guided meditation is to ignite your inner fire and keep your light shining brightly through the winter months.

Note to reader: Remember to take occasional long pauses to allow your tribe to visualize and go deeper into the meditation.

Get yourself in a comfortable position. Position yourself to sit up or lie down, whichever is most relaxing.

Close your eyes. Take a deep breath in and then release it. Allow your body to sink into the ground to prepare for deep relaxation.

Place a hand on your belly. Take a deep breath in and feel your belly rise. Hold for a count of three.

One.

Two.

Three.

When you exhale, pull your navel to your spine and push out any stale air you've been holding.

Let's do that again. Take a deep breath and hold it for a count of three.

Then release it completely by activating your abdominal muscles, pulling your navel to your spine as you blow out completely.

Place your mental focus on the soles of your feet. Imagine you have thick, healthy roots growing from the soles of your feet. Visualize roots burrowing through the ground and watch as they travel all the way to the center of the earth.

In the center of the earth there's a huge beautiful crystal cavern. In the center of the cavern, a huge glistening clear quartz crystal hangs from the ceiling.

The crystal was formed from healing waters containing ancient codes of wisdom.

Visualize wrapping your roots three times around the crystal.

One.

Two.

Three.

See and feel the beautiful white crystal energy flow like a river, traveling up through your roots, through the earth back to the ground beneath you, and into the bottom of your feet.

Watch as the white light flows up your spine, to your heart space, your throat space, to your third eye, to the crown of your head and spout out the top of your head into the space above you.

Note to reader: *Pause here for a minute.*

Visualize the river of white light energy as it activates circulation up and down your spine. Watch as it lights your entire body with white healing light.

Breath in. Breath out.

Place your focus on the top of your head, your crown chakra. Notice it tingle as blood circulates. Notice how it feels when you place your attention on it.

Use your mind's eye to look above your head, high in the sky and see the glowing orange fire of the sun.

Imagine the sun's orange fire energy penetrating the crown of your head. Feel the sun's heat as it activates your fire within.

Visualize the bright orange light and warmth traveling from the top of your head to the center of your eyes. Notice how it fills you with light and warmth.

See the orange glowing fire travel to your throat chakra, lighting up its path with beautiful orange color. Watch it travel to your heart chakra, filling your heart space with bright light.

The light now travels to your solar plexus right above your navel. Then it travels to your abdomen below your naval.

Notice the warmth as it travels to the bottom of your spine, down your legs to your feet. Watch as the fiery orange light shoots from the soles of your feet. Breathe in, breathe out.

Notice your body tingle with the energy of the fiery light from head to toe. Visualize your entire body light up with bright, fiery orange light.

Breathe in, breathe out.

Visualize bright white energy from the beautiful crystal flowing upward from the earth into the bottom of your feet and up your spine.

See the sun's fiery orange energy wrap around the crystal's white light water energy, forming a double helix.

In your mind's eye see these two energies dancing together other up and down your spine.

Notice how the orange light and the white light wrap around each other like two pieces of thick rope.

Feel the two energies shooting up and down your spine, wrapped around each other in unity. Feel the activation of fire and water energies within you.

Now take a deep breath in and blow it out completely.

Breathe in the feeling of balance, love, strength, and harmony. Take one last breath in and gently blow it out.

Take your time getting up. Wiggle your toes and your fingers.

Remain in this state of activation and relaxation as long as you can. Gently open your eyes.

We are complete.

Burn/Destroy Your Release Paper

Guide your tribe to destroy the journal exercise #1 paper, including the trigger they wish to release. This can be done either by safely burning the paper, or by tearing it up and throwing it in a trash can. Before destroying it, guide your tribe to tell themselves, "I now release the trigger I no longer wish to hold onto."

Closing the Sacred Circle

You may pass the talking stick around and ask if anyone wants to share the trigger they released, or if they want to share the impact meditation had on them. Assure everyone that what is shared in the circle is sacred and will be kept confidential.

You may want to share first to help others get comfortable enough to talk. When someone shares, listen without comment. Thank them for being vulnerable and then ask the circle if anyone else wants to share.

Close the circle by guiding everyone to hold hands and lead a simple prayer of gratitude:

"We are grateful for this time of healing. We appreciate the love and open minds of the women here right now. We commit to bringing energy activation into the world when we leave the ceremony today. Let's all close our eyes and smile as you think of one thing that you're grateful for right now."

Thank everyone for coming. Tell them to take their time as they gather their things.

Remember to close your sacred space at the very end. You may do this by simply saying, "Sacred space now closed," or by reciting the Four Winds invocation offered in an earlier section of this book.

Be sure to smudge yourself from head to toe, letting go of any unwanted energy you may have picked up during the ceremony.

Extra Special

You can add to the experience by gifting each person a symbol of the season, such as a mini pumpkin, a small quartz crystal, a sunflower, anything that grows in season this time of year, or something that symbolizes fire such as a candle, firework, or sparkler.

You may add a special group prayer for someone in need, or for someone who is ill or suffering. Or you may say a group prayer for the world.

Invite them to pull an oracle card before leaving. Play uplifting energizing music as people gather their things and prepare to leave. End with playful dance music and invite everyone to dance to a song or two. Give each person a hug and tell them what you love about them.

Use your imagination and creativity to add your own personality to this ceremony. Trust your ideas, as they come from a higher source.

CHAPTER 18
NOVEMBER MOON: ACTIVATE YOUR CREATIVITY

Full Moon Ceremony – Activate Your Creativity

Intention: To activate your creativity by opening your "third eye" and stimulating action to manifest what you dream of.

Humans are creation machines. We create the world around us through intentions and by taking deliberate action. We create our families and our communities; we create our fun and literally everything in our lives.

Take a moment and think about something you've been wanting to create. It could be an art project, something you want to build, someone you want to become, a book you want to write, or a family you want to have.

Now ponder for a moment about what might be holding you back from the creation you desire. We unknowingly hold ourselves back from creating our dreams by saying yes to the wrong things.

There is a universal law called the Law of Sacrifice, which says, "In order to create and attain something you greatly desire, you must give up something of lesser value."

For example, if you want to have a better relationship with someone you love, then you have to give up something that gets in the way of that greater relationship.

If you want to write a book, create art, or improve your home, you have to give up another activity to make time for it. If you want to become a leader in your field, you have to give up being in your comfort zone. If you want to get your body in shape, you have to give up lounging on the couch and eating ice cream, and you have to replace it with exercising and eating healthy.

For me, every time I commit to writing a book, I have to give up sleeping late and wasting time on social media in the morning. It's a temporary sacrifice, but it's necessary to finish my book.

The Law of Sacrifice is very clear: you must say no to something that's in the way of creating something else you desire more.

Set Your Sacred Space

Prepare your sacred space as directed in the How to Use This Book chapter. Clear your sacred space of any unwanted energy. Call in your guides and higher self to bring positive energy to the space. Ask your guides, "Please provide me with the wisdom to create a powerful experience for the women who attend. Help me guide them to open their third eye and activate their creativity. Allow me to be the light and raise their vibrations."

Welcome

Welcome your tribe into the space, one by one. Thank each person for being here. Make each one feel loved and special. Put your index finger gently into each person's third eye area (the space between the eyebrows) and say, "We're going to open up your third eye tonight." Clear each woman's energy as she enters. Invite her to find her space and get comfortable.

Opening

Open with a sound, chime, gong, or any audible indication that it's time to begin.

Ask everyone to become fully present. Help them settle in by asking them to take one deep breath in, hold it, and slowly release it completely.

Give a loving smile and tell your tribe what tonight's intention is, then begin the ceremony. Remind everyone that this is a safe space and anything shared in the circle is to be kept confidential.

In this ceremony we will:

1. **Get clear** on what you want to create.
2. **Identify** what you've been saying yes to that gets in the way of what you want to create.
3. **Inspire** new choices by saying no to what holds you back and saying yes to true desires.

You may choose to pass the talking stick around the room and ask each woman to say their name and introduce themselves.

Another option is to invite each person to say their name and tell one thing everyone loves about them. This exercise is a beautiful way to help women embrace what is lovable about themselves by inviting them to look at themselves through the eyes of those who love them.

You may choose to either read the introduction to this chapter or tell a story about yourself or someone else who broke through a creative block by opening their mind and shifting their point of view.

Journal Exercise

Make sure everyone has two small pieces of paper and a pen. Guide them through this exercise, allowing five minutes for each step.

Prepare for journaling by guiding everyone to close their eyes as they take one deep breath in and blow it out audibly (making a "whew" sound as they blow out). Then take another deep breath in and blow it out completely. Lastly, take a breath in and blow it out. This breathing exercise helps tap into your higher knowing for a better journaling experience.

Journaling Exercise #1: Get Clear Write three things you wish to create in your life. Examples: A creative project, a relationship, something for your health, a lifestyle, etc. (This paper will be reserved and kept as a reminder.) Circle the one creation most important to you. This is the one you will commit to first. Next, write one action you will take to show you're committing to this creation. Example: "I will sign up for a gym membership," or "I will buy supplies for my project," or I will tell my loved ones, "I'll be working on this project for __ hours each day," and ask for their support.

Journaling exercise #2: Identity and Release Write down one to three things you've been saying yes to that prevents you from creating the most important creation you circled. Those things can be actions (doing too much for other people's dreams), thoughts (putting yourself down, fears and doubts), or habits (waking up late, eating too much) that hold you back.

(This paper will be burned or destroyed at the end of the ceremony.)

Meditation

Note to reader: Take long pauses in between each visualization segment. Moments of silence will allow your tribe to better ease into the meditation.

We're going to get you very relaxed and grounded. Then I will lead you to visualize using your imagination to enter more powerful states of receiving.

Allow your body to get in a very comfortable position, either lying down or sitting up. Close your eyes. Take a long deep breath in, then release it slowly.

Allow the muscles around your eyes to relax, and your body to sink into the earth, settling into deep relaxation. Relax the muscles in your forehead. Feel your skin tingle as it releases tension from the day.

Relax your face and unclench your jaw muscles.

Take a deep, cleansing breath in.

Release it completely by pulling your naval into your spine.

Take another deep breath in, then release it completely by zipping your belly button into the back of your spine. Release more air than you took in; this cleanses your energy centers.

Now, breathe naturally and notice how your belly rises and falls with each inhalation. Place one hand on your sacral chakra, the area of your abdomen just below your belly button.

Notice the warmth from your hand as it activates this energy center.

With your next inhalation, set the intention to send your breath directly to your sacral chakra, right where your hand is.

Notice your breath filling that energy center as your hand rises and falls.

Now I want you to imagine that you have a silver cord coming out of your belly button. Imagine that your body is very light like a balloon, and the cord is an anchor to keep you from floating away.

Now visualize the silver cord burrowing into the ground beneath you. Watch as it travels to the center of the earth where there is a huge oak tree.

Take the silver cord and wrap it around that oak tree three times.

One.

Two.

Three.

You are now grounded.

Move your attention to the space between your eyebrows, your third eye chakra. As you place your attention on the third eye, set an intention to make that spot tingle simply by putting your attention on it.

Notice sensations you feel at the third eye center as you place awareness on it.

Visualize the third eye located in the center of your head, between your eyebrows. Notice how your third eye looks exactly like an eye with an eyelid and eyelashes.

Stay focused on the third eye.

See it flutter open, as if it's been asleep for a long time.

See how wide you can open your third eye in your imagination.

What color is your third eye? How big is it? Does it shine brightly, or is it still sleepy?

Now look at the color of your third eye and look deeper. Can you see the cosmos in that eye? Try to visualize the cosmos swirling around it.

Your third eye is a receiver of information. When it's open it brings wisdom from the energy of *all that is*.

Now I want you to imagine that high in the sky above you there is a full moon glowing.

See the moon shine bright moonbeams directly into your third eye. Moonbeams carry the wisdom of the ages.

If you choose to receive this celestial wisdom, open your third eye wider to see the light shine brightly. Know that answers to everything are available to you right now.

As you take your next breath, breathe moonlight deep into the third eye and in your mind ask the moonlight this question: "What do I need to know right now?"

Now listen. The first thing that pops into your mind is always the right answer, no matter how simple it may be.

Note to reader: Pause for a minute here.

Take another breath in, and as you do, see the moonbeam get brighter. Now ask, "What do I need to say no to so I can say yes to something greater?"

Now listen. The first answer that pops into your mind is the right answer, no matter how simple it may be.

Now take another sip of breath. Watch the moonlight continue to shine in your third eye. Watch as the light expands to fill your whole head, then down to your throat chakra.

See the moonlight travel and light up your heart space. Now watch it continue to travel downward as it illuminates your body; see it light up your belly, your abdomen, your tailbone. Now watch as it lights up your entire body from head to toe.

You are now glowing and illuminated with this light. Now you are illuminated completely with the light and wisdom of the full moon.

If you have another question for the marvelous wisdom of the moon, ask it right now. Know that the first answer you receive, no matter how simple it may be, is always the right answer.

Note to reader: *Pause for a minute here.*

As you lie there illuminated, breathe in the feeling of peace.

Breathe in love, breathe in creativity. Take one final deep inhalation. Now release it completely by pulling your belly to your spine.

We are complete.

Sharing

If you desire, pass a talking stick around the circle and hand it to anyone who wants to share their thoughts, feelings, fears, and experience about journaling and meditation.

You can encourage sharing by going first. Share your own journaling answers with your tribe. The more authentic and honest you are, the more you will encourage others to share also.

Burn/Destroy Your Release Paper

Guide your tribe to destroy the journal exercise #2 paper, including those items they wish to release. This can be done either by safely burning the paper, or by tearing it up and throwing it in a trash can. Before destroying it tell yourself, "I now release these things I no longer wish to hold onto."

Closing

Close the gathering by guiding everyone in a simple prayer of gratitude. You may want to invite everyone to hold hands for added connection. Say something like this:

"We are grateful for this time of healing. We appreciate the love and open minds of the women here right now. We commit to spreading this beautiful energy into the world when we leave this ceremony today. Let's all close our eyes and smile as you think of one more thing you're personally grateful for right now."

Thank everyone for coming. Tell them to take their time as they gather their things.

Remember to close your sacred space at the very end. You may do this by simply saying, "Sacred space now closed," or by reciting the Four Winds invocation offered in an earlier section of this book.

Be sure to smudge yourself from head to toe, letting go of any unwanted energy you may have picked up during the ceremony.

Extra Special

You may add to the experience by inviting them to pull an oracle card before leaving. You may also add a special group prayer for someone in need, or for someone who is ill or suffering. Or you may say a group prayer for the world.

Gift each person a crystal, stone, or essential oil, anything that may be symbolic of the work done in this ceremony. Play uplifting energizing music as people gather their things and prepare to leave.

Use your imagination and creativity to add your own personality to this ceremony. Trust your ideas, as they come from a higher source.

CHAPTER 19
DECEMBER MOON: EXPAND YOUR HEART

Full Moon Ceremony – Expand Your Heart

Intention: Expand the love energy in your heart space and channel it to your throat chakra. Open your heart so you can transmit and express a higher love vibration into the world.

December is a time when many reflect on what was accomplished in the past year and assess how successful we were at hitting goals.

We tend to measure success in terms of how much money we made and how

much we accomplished. We were taught to measure success this way. It's how everybody does it; there's nothing wrong with it. However, there are other ways to measure success that are more meaningful.

In early 2022 I was faced with the most difficult challenge. My beloved husband Drew was dying in a hospital. Doctors told me he would not survive the ventilator and Covid-induced pneumonia. I stopped going to work, as I needed to be at the hospital all day, every day. For nearly five months, every hour was spent trying to keep Drew alive. Of course, our small business at the Brophy Art Gallery was impacted. It was mentally hard for me not to achieve the things needed to keep our business thriving. I was solely focused on bringing my husband home alive.

By December 2022, my husband was home and recovering from a medically induced coma, paralysis, learning how to walk, eat, and talk again. I was grateful for his miraculous survival! I also felt bad about myself for not finishing any significant work during the year. I shared my frustration with a friend who suggested I let my expectations go and flow with everything life was handing me.

I reflected on my ego's need to accomplish work projects, despite the near death of my husband. I realized how shallow that was. What good is success when the person you love is dying? The need for my ego to succeed during such a trying time got me thinking. What if we measured success based on something more meaningful, such as the amount of love and compassion we give each day?

After much thought, I made a decision: I would perform a minimum of three loving compassionate "good deeds" each day. This included being extra kind to someone who's hard to be around (because it's easy to give love to someone who is wonderful). It's the difficult personalities that challenge us the most.

The very next morning the Universe threw me a test. I walked outside and a longtime neighbor cornered me and complained about my fence. Immediately, my stomach ached. This neighbor is very negative, and in every conversation I have with her, she throws toxic energy all over me. I usually avoid her, as do the other neighbors on the street.

But on this particular morning, I decided not to run away from her. I asked myself, "What would happen if I gave her love and compassion right now?"

That was indeed a challenge! I discovered it would be easier to do if I looked for positive aspects about her. As she rattled on with complaints, I looked into her eyes and saw traits I never noticed before. She had beautiful green eyes and as I looked deeper, I saw the glimmer of a beautiful soul there.

As I focused on giving her love energy, I became fully present. I honored her by listening. I stopped resisting and surrendered. I smiled and offered silent compassion as I realized the poor woman had no idea why people avoided her.

Then I saw that giving love rather than the opposite felt *good!* My stomachache disappeared, and she responded to my loving vibration by softening her words. Our interaction ended on a high note.

Since then, I've been practicing giving love to everyone I interact with. I shoot for a minimum quota of three per day. The only way to be more loving is to practice it daily. Just like brushing your teeth—over time it becomes a habit.

Giving love in the form of compassion, listening, and offering help cultivates loving vibration in your being, making everything else in your life flow easier.

When we have a loving vibration, good things come more easily. People are kind in return and life flows better.

Set a daily love-and-compassion quota for yourself for the next thirty days. See how it changes your vibration and the world around you.

Set Your Sacred Space

Prepare your sacred space as directed in the How to Use This Book chapter. Clear your sacred space of any unwanted energy.

Call in your guides and higher self to bring positive energy into the space. Ask your guides, "Please provide me with the wisdom to enable the women here today to tap into their love and compassion. Help me give them exactly what they need at this time so they can spread it into the world. Allow me to be the light and raise their vibrations."

Welcome

Welcome your tribe into the space, one by one. Thank each person for being here. Make each one feel loved and special by offering a compliment, a hug, or a personal greeting. Tell each one, "I'm so glad you're here." Clear each woman's energy as she enters. Invite her to find her space and get comfortable.

Opening

Open with a sound, chime, gong, or any audible indication that it's time to begin.

Ask everyone to become fully present. Help them settle in by asking them to take one deep breath in, hold it, and slowly release it completely.

Give a loving smile and tell your tribe what tonight's intention is, then begin the ceremony. Remind everyone that this is a safe space and anything shared in this circle is to be kept confidential.

In this ceremony we will:

1. **Choose** how we wish to express and send love into the world.
2. **Release** the notions that hold us back from expressing love.

You may choose to pass the talking stick around the room and ask each woman to say their name and to introduce themselves. Another option is to invite each person to say their name and tell one thing that everyone loves about them. This exercise is a beautiful way to help women embrace what's lovable about themselves by inviting them to look at themselves through the eyes of those who love them.

Journal Exercise

Make sure everyone has two small pieces of paper and a pen. Guide them through this exercise, allowing five minutes for each step.

Prepare for journaling by guiding everyone to close their eyes and take one deep breath in and blow it out audibly (making a "whew" sound as they blow out). Then take another deep breath in and blow it out completely. Lastly, take a breath in and blow it out. This breathing exercise helps us tap into our higher knowing for a better journaling experience.

Option to Call in Your Guides

You may choose to invite the women to call in their higher self and their guides that are present for their highest good. Ask them to close their eyes, and repeat the following invocation in their minds as you read each line:

"Higher self, please join me here now and show me what I need to see."

Next, have them call in their spirit guides. Say, "If you know who your guides are, call them in by name. Some people call in Jesus, archangel Michael or other angels, a goddess, or their ancestors."

If you don't know who your guides are then mentally say, "To my spirit guides who are here for my highest good, please join me now and show me what I need to know."

Give them a moment of silence to mentally call their guides in.

"Take a deep breath. Feel confident that you're well-supported by your higher self and your spirit guides."

Journaling Exercise #1: Choose Write three ways you choose to show love and compassion for others. This can include giving compliments, cooking for loved ones, giving someone money or gifts, giving your time to someone in need, offering forgiveness when someone hurts you, etc. (This paper will be reserved and kept as a reminder.)

Journaling exercise #2: Release Take a few minutes to contemplate what has held you back from fully expressing love and compassion. Write three reasons you've held back love—people you know or strangers. Is it anger? Jealousy? Shyness? Is it that you're not sure how to show love or compassion? Are you afraid of giving too much? Take a moment and notice what comes up, then write it down. (This paper will be burned or destroyed at the end of the ceremony.)

Meditation

Note to reader: Take long pauses in between visualization segments. Moments of silence allow your tribe to better ease into meditation.

I invite you to get your physical body into a very comfortable position. Close your eyes. Take a deep cleansing breath in. Blow it out completely by pulling your belly button to your spine as you exhale.

Now, place a hand on your belly. Notice how it rises and falls with each breath in and out. Breathe in, breathe out.

Relax the muscles in your forehead. Relax your eyes. As you breathe out, relax all the tension in your jaw.

Let go of any clenching you may have in your facial muscles. Allow your face and neck to relax.

With each breath, feel yourself sink deeper and deeper into relaxation. Now visualize a thick, strong root growing from the base of your spine.

In your mind's eye, watch as the roots travel from the bottom of your spine into the ground, going deep into the center of the earth.

Now notice a large clear quartz crystal in the center of the earth, the size of a giant tree. See the crystal glowing brilliant bright white light. Now wrap your roots around the crystal three times.

One.

Two.

Three.

. . .

Feel the crystal's light energy travel up your roots and up to the base of your spine. As the energy travels upward, visualize it lighting your spine from your tailbone all the way up to your neck, then up to your third eye and out the top of your head.

Visualize your entire body emanating this beautiful white light. Breathe in that light. Breathe it out.

Place one hand on your heart space located in the center of your chest, between your breasts. This space is your transmitter, which houses your vibration and transmits that vibration to the world outside you.

Take a moment to notice what your heart's vibration feels like.

As you place your attention on your heart space, notice physical body sensations in that space. Feel your heart's vibration.

With your mind's eye, look in your heart space and see how open your heart is. Take a deep breath in, and as you do open your heart space wider.

Take a moment to notice and honor your heart space where it is right now.

Notice your heart's dark edges. Notice its scars. If you choose, feel into the sadness of those dark spaces and scars. It's okay to feel it. Honor whatever feelings come to you.

With your next breath mentally say, "I now release this." Take another breath in and breathe it out.

Note to reader: Observe a minute of silence here.

Place your mind's attention back to your heart space. Notice a light glowing in your heart. See with your mind's eye how the light in your heart overpowers the dark edges.

Visualize the light in your heart getting brighter with your next inhalation. As you breathe out, see the light glow even brighter. In your mind, say, "Heart, I love and accept all of you."

Note to reader: Observe a minute of silence here.

With your next breath in, see your heart space light glow so brightly it fills your entire body from head to toe.

See your entire body glow, bathed in its own love as you continue to breathe in and out.

Now, say to yourself mentally, "I love and accept my scars. I love and accept my light. I love and accept my love."

Note to reader: Observe a minute of silence here.

Now, visualize a golden thread attached to your heart space, and see it run all the way up to your throat chakra. This golden thread expresses your heart's vibration through your words and deeds.

Imagine your golden thread is vibrant, glowing, and lit up with the bright energy of your heart.

See that energy flood into your throat chakra, and allow it to express itself by putting a tiny smile on your face. Feel the energy of your heart in your smile.

Note to reader: Observe a minute of silence here.

You have now activated both your heart and throat chakras, expanding your love into physical expression.

Let's take one last healing breath in. Breathe it out.

We are complete.

Sharing

If you desire, pass a talking stick around the circle and hand it to anyone who wants to share their thoughts, feelings, fears, and experience with journaling and meditation. You can encourage sharing by taking the first turn. Share your own journaling answers or a story of your own experience that fits this theme.

Burn/Destroy Your Release Paper

Guide your tribe to destroy the journal exercise #2 paper, including those items they wish to release. This can be done either by safely burning the paper, or by tearing it up and throwing it in a trashcan. Before destroying, tell yourself, "I now release these things I no longer wish to hold onto."

Closing

Close the gathering by guiding everyone in a simple prayer of gratitude. You may want to invite everyone to hold hands for added connection. Say something like this:

"We are grateful for this time of healing. We appreciate the love and open minds of the women here right now. We commit to spreading this beautiful energy into the world when we leave this ceremony today. Let's all close our eyes and smile as you think of one thing you're personally grateful for right now."

Thank everyone for coming. Tell them to take their time as they gather their things.

Remember to close your sacred space at the very end. You may do this by simply saying, "Sacred space now closed," or by reciting the Four Winds invocation offered in an earlier section of this book.

Extra Special

You may add to the experience by inviting them to pull an oracle card before leaving. You may also add a special group prayer for someone in need, or for someone who is ill or suffering. Or you may say a group prayer for the world.

Gift each person a heart-shaped crystal, stone, essential oil, or anything that may be symbolic of the work done in this ceremony. Play uplifting energizing music as people gather their things and prepare to leave.

Use your imagination and creativity to add your own personality to this ceremony. Trust your ideas, as they come from a higher source.

CHAPTER 20
BONUS MEDITATION: CHAKRA-ACTIVATED INTUITION

Meditation to Activate Chakra Energy Centers

Intention: This meditation will activate our energy centers and deepen our intuition and inner knowing.

This meditation will activate our energy centers, which opens the path to go deeper into the power of our innate intuition, our inner knowing and our wisdom.

Meditation

I invite you to get your body in a comfortable position. You may do this lying down or sitting up. Close your eyes. Begin by taking three deep cleansing breaths.

Place your hand on your belly.

Breathe in and feel your belly rise with your breath.

Hold it for a count of three, two, one. Now release.

Take another deep breath in, and hold it for three, two, one.

Now release it completely by pulling your navel to your spine.

Take one more deep breath in through the nose, visualizing the breath traveling down your body and into your belly. Feel it rise, hold it, then release it completely by blowing out audibly.

Now let's get grounded in Mother Earth. Visualize roots growing from the bottom of your spine and your feet.

Watch as they burrow into the ground under the floor and travel all the way to the center of the earth, where there is a huge, beautiful crystal cavern.

In the center of the cavern is a large clear quartz crystal. Wrap your roots around the crystal three times.

One.

Two.

Three.

Now, place a protective bubble around your body. Visualize a golden light bubble all around you, as if you're sitting inside a golden egg. The golden light bubble is loving and soft. It powerfully protects you from any negative energies that don't serve you.

Now imagine a shower of liquid light raining on the top of your head from your crown chakra.

Visualize it pouring light energy into your crown and watch as the liquid light seeps down your head into your brow.

Watch as it illuminates your third eye chakra, the space in between your eyebrows.

See your third eye twinkle as light energy activates it to allow you to receive new knowledge.

Whisper to yourself, "I accept and embrace all wisdom that comes to me."

Take a deep breath to seal in that invitation.

Watch as the light energy pours down from your third eye into your throat chakra.

See the light energy brighten that beautiful butterfly in your throat, energizing your voice and the courage to speak your truth.

Take a breath in and enjoy the wonderful feeling of expressing freedom that liquid light activates within you.

Watch as the light moves into your heart chakra, that space in the center of your chest, right between your breasts.

As the light enters your heart chakra, see it light up a bright, beautiful green color.

Your heart is a transmitter of emotion and vibration. In your mind, ask the liquid light to help you to transmit love and emotions which will serve the highest good for everyone in your life.

Take a deep breath and watch as your heart chakra expands more, filling your entire chest with a beautiful green glow.

Now take one more breath and watch as your heart chakra expands beyond your protective bubble, filling the room with beautiful, loving green light. Take a breath to seal in the activation of your heart chakra.

See the liquid light move into the space above your belly button, your solar plexus. Breathe in the feeling of JOY, knowing that your life is completely in your hands.

Whisper to yourself, "I am perfect just as I am."

Take a breath to seal in the feeling of worthiness. Next the liquid light travels to the space below your naval, your sacral chakra. Watch as it illuminates your abdomen and activates your creativity.

Breathe in the freedom to create and to birth your ideas and dreams.

Whisper to yourself, "I am a creative being." Take a breath in to seal in the feeling of confidence in your own dreams.

Watch the beautiful golden liquid light melt down into the base of your spine, your root chakra. Visualize all the golden light pooling at the base of your spine, lighting your feeling of safety and stability.

As you take your next breath, whisper to yourself, "I am safe. The universe always provides for me. I always get exactly what I need."

Now imagine the liquid light traveling back up your spine, lighting up your sacral chakra. See it move up to illuminate your solar plexus, your heart chakra, your throat chakra, into your third eye and shooting through your crown chakra and out the top of your head into the heavens.

Take a moment to enjoy the high vibrations you just created within your sacred body.

You just activated your inner power, your ability to access your inner wisdom.

Seal this activation by taking a deep breath in, hold it for a few seconds, then release it.

We are now complete.

CHAPTER 21
BONUS MEDITATION: MANIFESTING A GOAL

Meditation to Manifest a Goal

Intention: This meditation will help manifest a goal you have been dreaming of bringing to life.

This meditation will help you get into the energy of manifesting a goal you've been dreaming of. This is a great meditation to do in spring or summer, or anytime when the time is ripe for giving life to your dreams.

Meditation

Get yourself into a comfortable position, either lying down or sitting up. Close your eyes. Take a deep breath in. Blow it out. Settle into your body, and notice your belly rise and fall with each breath.

Now, in your mind's eye, I invite you to visualize yourself standing in a large, beautiful garden. The garden represents your life. You are barefoot. Notice how the dirt feels on the soles of your bare feet.

See the sun high in the sky and feel its warmth on the top of your head. Place your attention on the soles of your feet. Imagine there are healthy roots growing from the bottom of your feet.

In your mind's eye see your roots burrowing deep into Mother Earth below us. Watch your roots travel all the way to the center of the earth, where there is a large cavern.

In the center of that cavern is a very large, very old wise oak tree. Imagine wrapping your roots three times around the thick trunk of the wise oak tree.

One.

Two.

Three.

Feel the earthly energy from the tree travel up your roots, into the soles of your feet. Feel it travel up your spine, all the way to the top of your head.

See the sun above your head as a bright, glowing ball of energy. Feel rays of sunshine on the crown of your head. See the bright light flood your head with a warm glow. See it travel down to your third eye, then into your throat space.

Now see the light travel down to your heart space, lighting up every inch of your body as it continues downward. See the light fill your belly, your sacral chakra, and your base chakra at the bottom of your spine.

Allow the light to fill you completely.

See your body glow with this beautiful light. Look at your garden and notice the plants you've been growing most of your life. Each plant represents something or someone in your life that you love.

Take a moment and feel appreciation for yourself for figuring out how to grow these things that you love. Honor the you from the past, the you who planted this garden. Thank yourself for the good work you have done. Breathe in the feeling of appreciation for yourself. Breathe out.

Notice at the side of your garden there is a clear space of fresh soil, ready for planting new things that you love. Walk over to the soil and kneel down. Notice a tray of fresh baby seedlings to your right, ready to be planted in your new garden.

Each baby seedling represents your dreams and goals. Choose one of the goals you wish to plant and nurture today. Reach into the tray and pull out the baby seedling representing your chosen goal. Dig a hole to plant it in your garden, and lovingly place it into the soil. Gently cover the roots with dirt.

Now, look up to the sky and ask the heavens to rain on it. Watch as rain moistens your seedling. See it grow taller into a small green stalk, shooting up from the dirt. Now call to the sun to nourish it.

Watch the sun's rays illuminate your seedling and watch the vibrant green shoot grow taller into a beautiful green plant.

Take a moment to imagine what your goal will look like in real life when it's fully manifested. Imagine how you will feel. Visualize the impact.

See what you'll be doing when the goal comes to life. Walk closer to your baby plant. Ask the sun to keep it warm.

Whisper to your plant that you love it.

Say in your mind, "I love you. I nurture you. I have patience and will enjoy watching you grow."

Feel good knowing that you will enjoy the beauty of the process of bringing your goal to life.

Put a smile on your face. We are complete.

CHAPTER 22
ONE MOON AT A TIME

Take This Work Into the World, One Moon at a Time

This book is meant to inspire and encourage you to start your own women's circles, to spark the light in your own community.

I invite you to start today, wherever you are. You are ready. Put a date on the calendar, reach out to the women you know and invite them. Make your first one happen now.

Take this work into your world, one moon at a time. With each passing moon, you will grow the sisterhood stronger and stronger. As you do, you will expand into your greater purpose as well.

You can begin with two or more people. Over time, it will grow as word gets out. People need healing more desperately than you can imagine. Some will attend and won't even know why they did until much later when they see the results of self-empowerment.

Invite your sisters, your mother, daughters, and friends. Invite your neighbors and community. Have fun with it. Don't strive for perfection; strive to make each woman feel loved in your presence. That's the main goal. Anything that comes in addition is a bonus.

It is my intention that the contents of this book will make it very easy for you to lead a woman's circle. After a few months of practice, you may begin to trust your intuition, higher guidance, create your own meditations and writing exercises, or you may continue to use mine. Either way, the work you do with this concept will be very important.

With great love,

Maria

P.S. Please connect with me in real life. I would love to hear your feedback about how this book helped you create a sisterhood in your community. You can message me through the following online platforms:

Join my Inner Circle and get free resources here: https://mariabrophy.com/circles

Instagram @MariaBrophy

Youtube https://www.youtube.com/@mariabrophy1

My online courses www.BrophyArtAcademy.com

MESSAGES FROM SISTERS OF THE MOON COLLECTIVE

Andréa Christine:

The "success" of an event relies solely on creating an environment where everyone feels safe to express themselves, safe to relax their nervous system, and safe to feel whatever they are feeling inside.

A message from Sisters of the Moon Collective co-founder Andréa Christine:

"Maria has been my friend for years. I was fortunate to meet her in Egypt. How could we not expect to create magic together?

One of the most memorable compliments I've ever received was from Maria during one of our full moon events. One night after she led a guided meditation, she watched as I crafted sound healing music, moving swiftly from crystal bowls, to my gong, and to other instruments. Later she said to me, "You're like a brilliant, mad scientist!"

Sometimes I feel we're all mad scientists or alchemists. We have amazing opportunities to "experiment" with ever-changing states of experiences and emotions, identifying gifts of growth along the way. The ultimate goal is to simply enjoy life on this beautiful planet and share as much love as possible.

I've been practicing sound therapy, doing energy work and movement facilitation for over a decade. Through my study with brilliant teachers, I've learned that the physical body holds immense amounts of energy and memory. Sometimes it truly "takes a village" to support releasing stuck energy and reinforce new positive patterns. Sound and movement can be two of your best allies, and shared in community their healing effects are amplified. Our ancestors knew this well.

For those who haven't experienced a sound bath, here's a simple explanation. Relax and allow the vibrations of different instruments to wash over you. The harmonic experience brings coherence and peace as you relax mind and body. As beings made of mostly water, humans are impressionable to vibration. From time to time it's a good idea to allow a little tune-up. This could be a series of deep conscious breaths, a mini-meditation in the grocery store, or a sound bath.

A major lesson I've learned from holding space for others is the value of releasing expectations of how something *should be,* and just embracing the flow. This honors divine feminine energy flowing free like water by receiving a state of power rather than force. As long as there is conscious intention and integrity through preparation, life is good.

Another lesson is safety first! The success of an event relies solely on creating an environment where everyone feels safe to express themselves, safe to relax their nervous system, and safe to feel whatever they are feeling inside. We facilitate a safe space for participants to process emotions, smile, remember who they are, and leave the dance floor feeling renewed!

Thank you, Maria, for the opportunity to contribute to your book and co-create magic with you in this lifetime. Through attention and intention to healing, and with community support and the tools offered in this book, we help bring balance and harmony back to our beautiful planet Earth.

May the energy of this book inspire all who read it to tap into their unique gifts and create magic individually and in community. The world can always use more magic.

In love and gratitude,

Andréa Christine

Thank you for tuning in! If you're interested in learning more about what I do, please visit *www.andreachristine.space* and follow me on Instagram at @andreachristine369.

Christine O'Donnell

"The more we connect with nature's cycles and the moon's magic, we find balance within mind, body, and spirit."

A message from Sisters of the Moon co-founder Christine O'Donnell:

Hello beautiful souls! My name is Christine. I am a Reiki master and co-founder of Sisters of the Moon. Full moon ceremonies have been part of my journey for many years, and I am so grateful to have the opportunity to share this ancient wisdom with the Sisters of the Moon community. During our gatherings, I guide intention setting through a journal exercise highlighting the zodiac signs of the full moon. I also share Reiki energy healing.

Mama Luna is the heartbeat of the cosmos in direct connection with the Earth. The moon represents divine feminine energy, while the sun represents divine masculine energy. Think of this as yin and yang creating balance in our lives. The moon also universally represents the flow of a woman's cycle. The moon takes 29 days to complete its lunar cycle, and women's menstrual cycles are generally 28 days.

Her rhythm vibrates to the oceans and waters within us. The full moon's energy is so powerful it influences ocean tides, creating what surfers call king tides. If the moon affects our oceans representing 70% of the earth's surface, and humans are 70% water, then the moon affects us too!

When the moon is full, it illuminates wisdom, shining light on us and stirring emotions beckoning us to go deeper within. The full moon is an auspicious time in the lunar cycle, inviting us to meet our souls in deep reflection and self-inventory. This time in the lunar phase is an optimal for reflection to help let go, forgive, and shed what no longer serves us.

The moon constantly flows in a dance around the earth throughout the zodiac wheel. Every two-and-a-half days the moon enters a different zodiac sign. Since there are twelve zodiac signs in the astrology calendar, we see the full moon land in a different zodiac sign every full moon. The moon also reflects our personalities, our inner world, and intuition. Therefore, the zodiac signs play a crucial part in the theme and personality of the moon every month. When we know which zodiac sign the moon is in, we understand what the moon teaches about our inner world, an opportunity to create more balance in our lives. To find out what zodiac sign the moon resides in, simply Google or download apps like, "The Moon" to find the sign the moon is currently in.

Every zodiac sign represents a different element of nature: fire, air, water, and earth. Observing zodiac signs and elements for each full moon ritual allows deeper connection with ourselves to let go and take action in our soul's journey. When we remember the elements of nature, we remember our connection to nature and realize we are not separate from it.

The element of fire symbolizes release. You can write an intention for what you want to release and safely burn the paper outside. Fire encourages ignition of the internal spark within to take action on goals or situations in our lives.

The element of air symbolizes change. Air inspires us to dance, move our sacred bodies, and create more space in our lives.

The element of water symbolizes formlessness and detachment. Water and the moon represent infinite flow and transformation of self.

The element of earth symbolizes stability, balance, and harmony. Earth grounds and roots us to nurture relationships with others and nature.

The more we connect with nature's cycles and the moon's magic, we find balance in mind, body, and spirit.

If you're interested in learning more, please connect with me at *www.ChristineEODonnell.com* or on *Instagram @Christine_e_Odonnell*

RESOURCES

Dear reader, I invite you to connect with me in real life, through the following platforms:

- My Inner Circle and free resources:
  https://mariabrophy.com/circles
- Instagram @MariaBrophy
- Youtube https://www.youtube.com/@mariabrophy1
- My online courses www.BrophyArtAcademy.com

Below are a list of websites and books I recommend to expand on the teachings in this book.

Recommended Books

Your Sixth Sense: Unlocking the Power of Your Intuition by Belleruth Naparstek

Creative Visualization by Shakti Gawain

The Success Sense by Candice Thomas

Art Money Success by Maria Brophy

The Celestine Prophecy by James Redfield

The Great Cosmic Mother by Monica Sjöö and Barbara Mor

Recommended Online Sites and Training

Daily Writing Practice with Maria Brophy (A 14-day meditation and journaling course) https://www.brophyartacademy.com/healing-arts

The Four Winds Society https://thefourwinds.com

Sisterhood tools and wisdom https://www.globalsisterhood.org/

Shamanic practitioner and teacher https://themoonandstone.com/

Intuition expert https://candicethomasintuitive.com/

BY MARIA BROPHY

Books

Art Money Success

Painting Surfboards Chasing Waves

90 Days to a Passive Income Stream

Living the Dream

How to Make Money Painting at Live Events

Audio

Art Money Success audiobook

Guided meditations on Youtube:

https://www.youtube.com/@mariabrophy1

Healing Arts Courses

Daily Writing Practice; 14 Days to Discovery and Joy

Sprouting the Seed of Life with Katie Doherty

All courses are at https://www.brophyartacademy.com/healing-arts

Social Media

Instagram @mariabrophy

Twitter @mariabrophy

Tiktok @mariabrophyart

Join my Inner Circle and get free resources here: https://mariabrophy.com/circles

Made in United States
North Haven, CT
22 August 2023

40625706R00091